Yes!

Words Are Wonderful.

How to be a Wordsmith early...

By DJ (Derrick D. Shortridge JR)

WOW Book Publishing™

First Edition Published by DJ (Derrick D. Shortridge JR)

Copyright © 2021 DJ (Derrick D. Shortridge JR)

ISBN: 9798713296315

WOW Book Publishing™

All rights reserved. Neither this book, nor any parts within it may be sold or reproduced in any form without permission.

No part of this book may be reproduced in any form or by any electronic or mechanical means including information storage and retrieval systems, without permission in writing from the author. The only exception is by a reviewer, who may quote short excerpts in a review.

The purpose of this book is to educate and entertain. The views and opinions expressed in this book are that of the author based on his personal experiences and education. The author does not guarantee that anyone following the techniques, suggestions, ideas or strategies will become successful.

The author shall neither be liable nor responsible for any loss or damage allegedly arising from any information or suggestion in this book.

Dedication

To my Grandparents, you were around at the genesis but have gone on ahead. For my parents who created an atmosphere in which I developed my love of words and the need to educate as I am being educated.

Table of Contents

Dedication 3
Table of Contents 5
A note from the Author 7
Foreword.. 9
Testimonials 11
Derrick D. Shortridge (DJ)... 13
Acknowledgements... 15
In the Beginning There Was the Word.... 17
A few actual Diary entries from 2015.................................. 19
YOUNG WORD WIZARDRY 101.. 23
Words Change Lives:... 25
    BABY CAN READ: 25
    BUSY BEES: 26
    Reception:... 26
Awesome Action Words!!! 31
WORDS TAKE SHAPE: 34
    Memories from my journal for the year 2016 36
    My birthday (not that long):... 40
    The Great Fire of London school play: 41
    Last Week of Year 1: 41
Nothing But Nouns: 43
    Noun Quiz: 45
A New Layer Of Words... 49
    A few actual diary entries by DJ in 2017 49

Table of Contents

A New Level of Words Resumed 55
    The Inky Ages: 55
ADVERBS AND ADJECTIVES: 56
    Actual Diary entries from 2017 – DJ age 7: 60
Different Words Have Similar Meaning: 60
Understanding punctuation and phrases 66
    PARENTHISIS: 67
Word journey level 5 ... What a Jive? 72
    A Few actual Diary entries from 2019 – DJ age 72
    IDIOMS, NOT IDIOTS! 86
ACRONYMS AND MNEMONICS! 89
Words Are Communication Tools: 91
    A few actual Diary entries from 2020 – DJ age 91
APOSTROPHES: 139
    IMAGERY: 139
    IMAGERY: 140
    Examples of Imagery: 140
Afterword by Derrick H. Shortridge Sr. 143
Some of my early work 145
NOTES: 152

A note from the Author

It was Nelson Mandela who said, *"All is impossible until someone does it."*

As I grew up and learnt to read and write, I found that literacy was a vehicle too sparsely used in life. My love for books and the spoken word developed from being exposed to tools like *'Baby can Read'*, an early gift from my parents. I interacted daily with my Mum, Dad and, older siblings which helped to shape my vocabulary immensely.

I wonder how many children do not have regular conversations with their siblings and parents? I suggest it is a vast number. It might be right to question, where did I find my fact...

Early Literacy is a tool that makes it easier for young people to learn to read. Having entered school with these skills has given me an advantage that I will carry with me for generations[1]. Reading is crucial for success in our education and in later life. I found truth from the fact that reading, rhyming, singing, and talking — beginning from birth — profoundly influences literacy and language development, the foundations for all other learning[2].

Dad taught me to write down my thoughts and daily episodes from an exceedingly early age. He insisted that I document my life events each day; he called it, journaling, I have been journaling for the past seven years... I think he called it journaling... I used a lot of those writings to inform my work on this

A note from the Author

project. Over the years I have gathered some wonderful facts about words, and I introduce them to you.

I have favourites like *'Wildlife of Britain'*[3], *'How is it done?'*[4] *'The Bible for Minecrafters'*[5], *'1001 Secrets every Birder should know: tips and trivia for the backyard and beyond'*[6]. Make connections between books you read and things you have done. I found out early that reading is not only about sounding out words but to make sense out of what we're reading.

Making connections to text through talking about an experience (something you have read before or watched on TV) help us as children to build our knowledge bank, for use throughout life, I reckon.

As children grow, we can become enthusiastic or fixated about particular subjects such as dinosaurs, trains, cars, football etc[7]. That interest can help your child to be similarly excited about reading both fiction and non-fiction books! We need to find and use libraires Dad took me to the library early and brought lots of books home from his tutoring business, sometimes 30 in 1 week.

Writing this book has been a joy and I think that if you finish reading and utilising the materials contained in it, if you are not inspired, you should read it again. I have reread several of my books; my parents sometimes question me about that - but words are my passion.

Don't quit reading!

Foreword

Dear Reader,

'Yes! Words Are Wonderful' is the book needed to read to help children, young and older folks to recognise the power of literacy. It is a tool that makes it easier for children and adults to learn to read.

Derrick Junior has acquired some masterful skills and knowledge, far beyond his years and he imparts it to you in a way that will allow you to understand and apply it immediately.

The knowledge in this book has the power to help you create a love for reading, along with understanding and using words with confidence. I can tell you that even with my experience as a successful author and internationally acclaimed speaker, I was amazed at his mastery of language when I met him at the WOW BOOK CAMP.

Derrick Jr. has the drive, heart and the developing expertise to become a successful author. I am pleased with his progress and confident he will be helping many of his peers and other people to read, use language and even write books in the extremely near future.

Vishal Morjaria
Award Winning Author
and International Speaker

Testimonials

"Derrick D. Shortridge (DJ) was born loving words. From his earliest days, books and reading have been DJ's passion, and this is clear to see in his book `Yes! Words are Wonderful.` It is part journal, part autobiography, part instruction manual, and fully a celebration of the literary journey of a talented young writer.

Encouraged by his father to start a journal at an exceedingly early age; DJ shares with us, incidents, and memories from his life. From haircuts and pet fish, descriptions of teachers and school friends, to family holidays and karate lessons.

All with a wonderfully direct and conversational style, giving us glimpses into the life of a young person growing up in East London. But DJ also talks directly to other aspiring writers; with hints, tips, grammar lessons and encouragement for other children to take up their pens or laptops - and start their own adventures in writing."

Guy Fairbairn
Head teacher

Testimonials

"DJ is an amazing young word wizard; he picks up writing techniques so quickly that I envy his talent as an author. I genuinely enjoyed working with DJ on this book as his Book Angel. I hope to see him continue to grow and inspire other young people to be as passionate about words and writing as he is."

Pauline Barath
Author and Book Angel

Yes! Words Are Wonderful.

Derrick D. Shortridge (DJ)
The young word wiz

Derrick D. Shortridge (DJ) is a ten-year-old boy, born in London to parents who are both educators in the East end of the city for over nineteen years. His mother is a primary school teacher and his father a secondary science department head for many years. DJ likes to say to himself that he was born in Jamaica as most of his family is from the famous Caribbean island. Derrick possessed a very wide-ranging vocabulary even from a tender age. His ability to hold a conversation as a baby astounded all who encountered him.

He was a young wordsmith; he could talk for England and Jamaica if given the opportunity. He represented his class and school in many events including but not exclusively, taking lead roles in school productions – Samuel Pepys in *'The Great Fire of London'*, swimming, debate, and multiple stints as a member of the learning council like a sort of status in his school during his time at Selwyn Primary school.

Having read many books from different genres, he has developed an appetite for various styles, but adventure and intrigue are what excites him most. DJ journaled from the time he was able to write his first letters. His Dad constantly reminded him of the need to capture and record events in his life as soon as possible after they happened.

Derrick has expressed interest in literacy, especially of young people and saw the need to write this book using his journal as the blueprint. He has added tools for developing grammar to it with a view to helping his peers, and children in general, develop a working knowledge of the English language.

He was adamant he would contribute to literacy in his school, academy trust, local authority, city, country and the world in a way that inspired parents and children. Derrick reads everything and realises that reading is a privilege not afforded to everyone and is honoured to contribute to the world by writing this book. As DJ said, *"After all, God put us on this earth to contribute to the world, so a book for the uneducated is a perfect way of doing my part."*

Acknowledgements

I would like to thank a great number of people starting with the creator God for loving me unconditionally. To my greatest influencers, my parents who loved, encouraged, and stood by me for as long as I have been around. Parents have such a great impact on children's development and you both showed that to me always.

To my bother Tore and sister Mitri, I love you so much. Thanks for just being there so I could have conversations and share my thoughts with you. To my wider family, my aunts, uncles, cousins, and friends, I thank you for your influence on me. To my Squad and wider school community I say a huge thank you for helping nurture confidence in my ability.

In the Beginning There Was the Word...

In the beginning, mankind started by writing letters on stones. This evolved from pictures to symbols which were combined to record messages and events. This later evolved to languages and dialects and eventually paved the road for the written word as we know it today.

It all started with single letters forming single words and now it's our daily practice to use the written word to record events by using descriptive and elaborate sentences. This book is a composite of the journal of one of these exceptional specimens, known as DJ!

Yes! Words Are Wonderful.

A few actual Diary entries from 2015

Thursday 24/12/2015

On Christmas Eve, I got a haircut at the *'Barbara's'* also known as barbers. Today, they were female. `Tony's barbers`, the name of… you guessed it… the barbers that I go to, has male and female barbers, and my parents and I have learnt that the female barbers are the best of their trade in the facility. MAN are their haircuts good!

Friday 25/12/2015

Today was Christmas day and I opened my fabulous presents! Christmas is the best time in the Shortridge house thanks to the top tier presents, taste in design, songs and a selection of gadgets that serve greatly as a source of blasting the best Christmas carols to have ever existed.

Monday 28/12/2015

Today we stayed at home because I couldn't pick up my fish at the pet shop. I had waited pretty much all my life to get a pet, but, unfortunately, it was delayed due to a little error. Dad forgot to plug in the filter in the fish tank. *"Never mind, DJ`,"* I thought. *"You'll pick them up on Wednesday."* I had decided on the names for them, too, which would be Swimsy and Swifty. As you can tell by that, I have enough positivity to serve the community.

Thursday 21/4/2016

Today was grading day once more. If you're not a karate student or only know the fake TV version, a grading is when you are tested to see if you can qualify for the next belt up. You can have gradings whenever you want, except for the penultimate or second-to-last belt because you must wait a year to achieve all the qualifications for the black belt grading. Now, I am finally an orange belt because before that was white with an orange stripe.

Thursday 5/5/2016

Today was my birthday! I am six, and, as six-year-olds do, I thought that I am a proper big boy now. Of course, nowadays, I feel that you're not a grown man or woman until you don't have to ask for permission to go to the toilet.

That's probably just me and it probably sounds like I'm a complete maniac or dunce, or both; take your pick but that's how I feel and you can't judge me – we don't judge here. After a day full of present-opening, squealing, eating and thanking, I was so tired that I fell asleep before my head hit the pillow when I went to bed!

Tuesday 7/6/2016

Mrs. Curtis told us today that she would bring a water tank in with eggs in it on Monday, so of course the whole class wouldn't be quiet about it from the time she said it until the time we were in our beds at home. Okay, maybe not that long.

Probably only until after we had our dinners; I, having a pet, was extremely interested in this announcement. When we enquired what they would be, she replied that they would be sea-monkeys, so my surprisingly vivid imagination instantly conjured up a picture of smallish monkeys in a tank with fins instead of arms swimming up to the edge of the tank miss talked about.

If you haven't seen the trailer for aqua dragons, then which rock have you been hiding under all this time? Then Sea-Monkeys are a hybrid breed of brine shrimp called Artemia NYOS invented in 1957 by Harold von Braun hut. Initially marketed as *'Instant Life,'* Sea-Monkeys are sold in hatching kits as novelty aquarium pets.

Yes! Words Are Wonderful.

YOUNG WORD WIZARDRY 101…

Yes! Words Are Wonderful.

Words Change Lives:

Greetings, dear reader! I am Derrick Daniel Shortridge, but you can call me DJ. If you have picked up this book to get your parents to stop nagging you about playing too many video games, then go away and find another book. WAIT!!! I am just kidding! If anything, it is even better for those of you who are bored, because I am here not to bore you even more, but to enlighten you. So, reader. Let me tell you a bit about myself...

BABY CAN READ:

At the tender age of about 1 or 2, my parents bought me a CD called "Baby can read". Let me tell you, that CD was such a blessing to my 1-year-old self that I felt like I was on the path to becoming a being of infinite knowledge. Even though the memory from the beginning of my journey is a little foggy, I still have some of the books to this day. And, since I presently and have always loved reading, we can safely assume that I probably read the books more than listened to the videos.

The basic principle of the books, of which I still have in my possession, is to show an image of, let us say... a tiger, then to write what the image is. I loved this, especially when they had little folds that you had to undo to see what the word is going to be. Trust me, it is endless amounts of fun for all the family ... if your family is made completely out of babies and toddlers.

Though I can barely remember it, one thing that stuck was the fact that all the babies on the videos were being smiled at by parents. May I add that I feel uncomfortable when adults just put on the fakest of fake smiles when trying to impress their demanding demon spawn *cough* I mean offspring.

BUSY BEES:

Fast-forward a couple of months and I went to a nursery called "Busy Bees", which was a lot of fun. Nurseries are one of the best words that has the letters I, E, and S after it because at a nursery, you get to: glue lollipop sticks to pieces of paper, an immensely popular activity for toddlers; throw glitter on everything, making you feel like the king or queen you are, run around until someone either gets sick or falls over and finally, sit in a circle and sing nursery rhymes.

The latter was one of the funniest things I could remember because quite a few of the children in the circle clearly were not that happy at the thought of not only being interrupted in one of the most intense games of tag they had ever had the experience of playing (back then, even eating could be an intense showdown) but being forced to sing `The Wheels on The Bus` 10 times over. Don't get me wrong, us children loved the songs back then. It's just that certain kids would sometimes throw a tantrum when we had to stop playing.

Reception:

When I had turned about four or five - this is a foggy memory, by the way - I went to what I think was the town hall with my Mum. We talked to a woman about what I now know was admissions to Selwyn Primary (well, mostly she asked questions and I only answered the man's questions).

Yes! Words Are Wonderful.

I remember this because she had a very cool bit of kit which, years later, my Dad told me was called a Newton's cradle, but back then, I just called a swingy-thingy; you know, the classic little child principle of wording. A few weeks later, my Aunt - Auntie Marcia - and I went to Selwyn Primary school; this was my first day in Reception.

Auntie Marcia had left and for the first five minutes, I thought to myself, 'OK. Cool. This is my life now.' Then, when I had internalized the fact that my own Aunt had just up and left, I started to cry. It was just a little whimper at first, but then the real waterworks came. Of course, Auntie Marcia did not just leave me there forever, but my five-year-old self just was not capable of comprehending that.

I thought that I was being abandoned. You see, that is a perfectly good reason for a so-called "big boy" to cry. Due to it being her job, Ms. Passat, who's the class teacher, came to my aid and read me a story. I think that is when my love of reading started to cultivate. The way books can transport you to magical lands full of cruel kings and nasty knights, or lands full of space creatures and futuristic technology, all from the comfort of your home fascinates me.

As the days progressed, I made new friends: Elon and Anthony. Those two put a spring in my step on the way to school in the mornings, making me want to get there even quicker. There was also my family. My Mum, Dad, aunts and uncles, (not all of them at the time, because there were some that I never knew existed) and everyone in between. I think reception was the year in which I felt most like I had a nice, clear path ahead of me. You know in those movies where one of the characters sees a remarkably simple path, which they start to travel along but becomes increasingly harder? That's pretty much people's lives. I know, I know. You are probably thinking, "man, this guy's just like my parents!" I will stop now.

By the end of the first week, I had 6 proper friends. They were Elon, Anthony (my first two Selwyn friends), Kacey, Kate, Ellie and Halley. Though we never really called each other the name until about year 4 (and by then Kate had left), we were the Selwyn Squad. Please do not close the book due to the phrase: I have lost many a reader due to that being (apparently) cheesy. I feel like it would be one of the pinnacles of common sense if I tell you all about the members of the Selwyn squad.

Elon:

Let us just say that he can get very over-excited easily, which can quickly turn to anger and rage. Usually, either Tommy (a later addition to the Selwyn Squad) or I are there to restrain him and calm him down, but on rare occasions, things can get awfully messy, awfully fast.

Anthony:

Anthony was as crazy as Elon sometimes, but could at least show some control over it. Even so, there are times in which he lets loose. He is German, though I have never heard him speak it to this day!

Ellie:

Ellie is a great friend you can count on to cheer you up and make you laugh. She has a stuffed elephant, which is her all-time favourite animal, named Jim, which is something she holds very dear.

Halley:

Halley is 1 of my only rivals when it comes to being the tallest in our year. She had been BFFs with Ellie since before they could talk. She also shares the same traits as Ellie. I have wondered many a time if they have a telepathic bond.

Kate:

Kate is a bubbly, cheery girl who loves to laugh. On many occasions, this has gotten me in trouble because her laugh is contagious.

Kacey:

Kacey must be the strangest female of all the previously mentioned members of the squad. She can make the stupidest of jokes without cracking a smile or laugh so hard that we cannot comprehend what she would say until she takes about 10 minutes of composing herself, which often led to another bout of laughter!

The terms progressed and I started to write reports of books I had read. I read books like "Chicken Licken" and, "the bad-tempered Ladybug". I would then draw a picture of what would be happening in the book, which I was immensely proud of.

Words Change Lives:

Yes! Words Are Wonderful.

Awesome Action Words!!!

Let's talk about 1 of the key parts of grammar. Verbs!

Verbs are words describing an action, state, or occurrence.

Examples of this are

- Run
- Eat
- Text

If you used it in a sentence, it would be used as

"Jeff ran through the streets to escape the tiny dog."

The word "run" is a verb because it is what Jeff was doing.

In certain cases, nouns (something I will explain later in chapter 1) and verbs could look the same.

For example, you could say,

"I am going out for a run".

In this context, "run is a noun because it is a thing.

If you said, *"Daniel ran",* that would be a verb because it is what Daniel is doing.

Here are some verbs that you can use in your writing:

Entry level Verbs - level 1:

- Run
- Sleep
- Jump
- Drink

Awesome Action Words!!!

- Go
- Move
- Eat

Moderate level Verbs – level 2:

- Text - To message people on a phone or other device
- Accomplished - To have done something
- Achieved - To get something that you aimed for
- Booted - To kick someone or something
- Obliterated – Another word for destroyed

Mastery level Verbs – level 3:

- Absconded – evaded
- Evaded – to get away from something
- Moderated – to lessen

Here's a quiz I prepared for you to have a go at now that you understand verbs.

Good luck!

1) What is a verb?

_____

_____

2) Is this sentence right or wrong?
   a. Why is it right/wrong?

The boy has eating a hotdog.

_____

Yes! Words Are Wonderful.

Verb detective

Help the |verb| detective.

- **Circle the verbs.**

walk
run
skip

The goddess Persephone lived in Ancient Greece. Her mother was the goddess Demeter, who made all the plants grow everywhere on Earth. In those days there was no winter or autumn. It was always spring or summer.
One day, when Persephone was playing in the fields, the ground opened. A deafening sound rumbled from the hole a chariot came roaring out. Dark horses pulled it. Hades, god of the Underworld was riding the chariot. 
Hades grabbed Persephone and took her to the Underworld to be his wife. The hole closed behind them.
Demeter looked all over the Earth for Persephone. She became so sad that she forgot all about the plants, so they did not grow. The first winter arrived.
Then a shepherd found Persephone's belt. He took it to Demeter.
"Where did you find it?" asked Demeter. The shepherd showed her. Demeter guessed what had happened. She told Zeus, the King of the Gods, "If you don't tell Hades to let Persephone go, I will stop making the plants grow. The Earth shall have nothing but winter."
Zeus ordered Hades to free Persephone. Demeter went to meet her, but Persephone could not leave the Underworld. She had eaten some pomegranate seeds. There was an old law about this. Anyone who had eaten in the Underworld had to stay there.
Demeter thought hard. A plan formed in her mind.

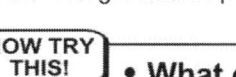 
- **What do you think Demeter did?**
- **Write three sentences about it.**
- **Circle the verbs.**

Teachers' note Remind the children of the different purposes of words in a sentence: to name people or things (or to use instead of these names), to show actions, to say where, when or why things happened and to show belonging. Tell them that they are going to investigate words for actions and introduce the term *verb* for these words.

100% New Developing Literacy
Sentence Structure and
Punctuation: Ages 7–8
© A & C BLACK

Managed to survive that? Good work!

33

WORDS TAKE SHAPE:

First things first, I am going to tell you about my teacher, Mrs. Sogi. Mrs. Sogi was a warm, open-minded teacher who made us all laugh. She was the kind of lady that you instantly felt comfortable around.

It was around this time that I started writing my sentences. In short, my sentences at that time were two or three sentences about my day. These were later used as things to look back on, from the perspective of whatever age I was, then compared to whatever age I would be when I read them over again.

In this year, the whole class developed a love of school trips. What are school trips, you ask? Well, school trips are outings you go on with your class to see lots of awesome places like the London Eye and the Science Museum. They are supposed to be educational, but let's get real; how is going to the science museum, touching the container of electricity, then giving your friends static shocks supposed to educate you?

I understood the concept of static shocks the same way I did before I entered the science museum than after I left it. Anyways, the first school trip of Year 1 was to this neat place called Butterfly world. Whilst there, not only did we see lots of different butterflies, but a wide variety of plants too. 1 of my all-time favourite butterflies, the monarch butterfly, was there and I told all my friends some facts about it, which included the fact that it travels from South America to New Mexico without once taking a break!

Here were also the marvelous carnivorous plants such as the Venus fly trap, which can die if you feed it chili pepper! In short, school trips are 1 of the best things about school.

Yes! Words Are Wonderful.

In that school year, I was an incredibly happy child. A lot of my playtimes consisted of chasing my friends around like we were mad people. Heck, we were and still are crazy! As Christmas drew near in December, I started to see Christmas lights hung up on people's houses. 1 of the houses that Mum and I were not at all surprised to see, was a house on Hurst Road, which, every year on around the 12th of December, had the most flamboyant Christmas lights in the history of flamboyant Christmas lights!

I also started my rock-hard belief in Santa. In fact, on the 19th of December, I wrote a couple - 5, to be exact - of letters to "Santa". I do not really believe in that stuff anymore now that I know who St. Nicholas is and the fact that none of my presents were ever labelled "To: DJ from: Santa". I mean, come on! If Coke (yes, the fizzy drink brand, not the thing you put in fires) had just left St. Nicholas alone, Santa wouldn't have been red! St. Nicholas was green originally! Do not ask me why I feel so passionately about Santa's mix-up because I honestly do not even know myself.

Christmas and Christmas Eve that year was as it was expected to be, if I'm being completely honest. On Christmas Eve, I went to the barbers with Mum, and at the time I had 1 of the best barbers I have ever had. In the Tony's Barbers shop, there was a woman whose name I cannot remember and those who left the shop about 2 years ago – 2018 who cut my hair like she was the goddess of barbers, which she probably was, to be fair.

Then, on Christmas Day, (before I describe it, please keep in mind that on these kinds of days, my sentences' information is very vague) I had lots of nice presents, along with some of Mum's delicious cooking. Let me tell you, my Mum and Auntie's food are the best of the best of the best of the… you get the picture. Their food is Top Tier!!

WORDS TAKE SHAPE:

Memories from my journal for the year 2016

The Christmas fun had faded, and I didn't really understand the concept back then, so not much really happened in the dying days of 2015. Then 2016 came around and I started to go to karate. Karate isn't about beating people to death, or looking epic and doing back-flips, which they do not even teach you in karate! If you want to learn that then you should go learn parkour. Jeez.

If you haven't shut this book to go find a YouTube video about how to do a backflip, then you should know that karate is all about discipline. In fact, most martial arts are about discipline. And although you can't use a Rasengan or Chidori (moves from Naruto) in real life, you can do some cool stuff. I really like karate because it makes you feel more at peace with yourself; causes you to far surpass your limits. Furthermore, it's tons of fun! I would recommend it to anyone who wants to learn a form of self-defence and have fun at the same time.

When Mum or Dad couldn't pick me up or drop me off at school, there was always Auntie Marcia or Kashief, who, at the time lived with us, to come to our aid. It's nice, having a family that you can depend on to help you out.

In the mornings, before I would go to school, I would do my times tables in a blue maths book unlike the ones you might have at school. I practised like crazy and watched the YouTube channel "Laugh Along and Learn", along with a channel called "Dr. DeMaio". Both channels focused on using famous songs, then altering the lyrics so that the song would recite the desired times tables.

Channel A (Laugh Along and Learn. Channel B is Dr. De Maio), however, focused mainly on songs for younger children, whereas Channel B focused mainly on the upper times tables

Yes! Words Are Wonderful.

(A.K.A 6 times tables and above) and more complex songs like "cheerleader". I would give it a 1000/10 for fun and 1000/10 for education. If it weren't for those two channels, I would probably be further behind than I am today and would have been then.

Nothing major happened until the 5th of March, my Dad's birthday. You know what's strange? Dad's birthday is the day before Mother's Day! Mum beat me twice in Ludo on the 10th of February, I had pancakes on most of the weekends, I loved my maths lesson, but not much really happened.

You know when, for long periods of time, every day seems to be a repeat of the previous? That was pretty much my life for 2 months. Then, on Dad's 49th birthday, I decided to give him a nice little treat in the form of breakfast in bed. Later in the day, we went to a restaurant and had some delicious Chinese-style delicacies.

Then, on Mother's Day, I made sure that Mum had the best quality comfort that I had to offer. I made a great card for her, covered in hearts. It had to be one of my best pieces of work so far!

Another dry zone came along up until the 15th. At the end of the school day on the 15th, the class was given the news that tomorrow is the 5-parts relief day. Then, on the 16th, we ran 1 mile in support. Elon, Anthony, and I stayed ahead of our class for most of the run, and we pretended we were running from a zombie apocalypse. You know, just your average Wednesday, getting chased by your class, all of which have been zombified, all while supporting good causes!

On Easter Sunday, I looked after Mum due to her feeling a little under the weather. Later in the day, I watched a movie with her called `Hop`, which is about a gutsy little rabbit who wants to become a pro at playing the drums. However, his Dad, the

Easter Bunny HIMSELF, wants him to take his place as the Bunny Supreme (just brainstorming some names for the Top Bunny which is 100% not a pun). Trying to improvise, E.B meets a man who had always wanted to become the Easter Bunny, then tries to show him the ropes.

Meanwhile, back at the ranch, things do not go too well at the Easter Bunny Factory.

An overgrown, overweight chick tries to take over the role of the Easter Bunny and turn it into the Easter Hen. Luckily, E.B and Fred - the E.B in training - bust through into the factory and gives the oversized chick "what for" by tricking him into jumping into a vat of hot chocolate. It's a great movie and I would recommend it to anyone who has even a tiny sliver of any humour-related sense.

Fast forward to the 23rd of March and I was taking my grading to become a… white belt orange stripe! For the first time, Mum took me to the grading instead of Kashief or Dad. We went to a supposedly humongous youth centre and used the sports hall in there. I have noticed that all the karate gradings that I had been in were in youth centres. The karate lessons that I usually do are in the paradox centre, which is also used for a youth club, dancing and a few other things besides.

I was a bit nervous when I had to stand up and go through my kata which is a certain series of moves, but that was stemmed by the fact that Mum was there, cheering me on. Nowadays, I don't get nervous. I just feel a wave of excitement. Currently, I am a brown belt with a white stripe, meaning that there are only three more belts until I am a black belt.

… Interesting things that happened up until my birthday the 5th of May ….

Yes! Words Are Wonderful.

On the 6th of April, I had finally learned my 6 times table. As you would expect for a 5-year-old, I was over the moon with joy, and in fact kept reciting it repeatedly on the way to school until I had branded it onto my brain. I was and still am a maths lover, so you would kind of expect me to be so pumped about this.

We had something called "French Day" at our school on the 8th of April, something I forgot had existed until I read through my sentences. Apparently, it's when all our lessons have something to do with France. Also, our French lesson would be double the length.

In topic, we learnt about; the Chrysler Building is still the tallest brick building in the world. The Chrysler Building was also the tallest structure in the world from 1930 to 1931. Before it was built, the tallest structure in the world was Eiffel Tower.

My cousin Kaion had his birthday on the 12th of April. We went to his party, which was "Star Wars" themed, and I was one of the pilots of the jet fighter that was called the millennium falcon. Fun times!

I had my grading again on the 21st of April. I became an orange belt, which was a bit ironic because I had an orange before I had left the house with Kashif to go to my grading. Oh, the irony!

Janay's birthday was on the 23rd. We went to a Chinese restaurant and, let me tell you, I was bloated when we went home!

WORDS TAKE SHAPE:

My birthday (not that long):

Today was indeed my 6th birthday and I being hell-bent on making it the best day of the year... aside from all the other awesome things that happened. I got lots of new books, lots of kisses, and a Lego set! This was a helicopter with water-ski add-ons. There was also a prison to build and a couple of trees. This would last me for a long time! You would not have known me then, but anything like a Lego set would interest me for hours upon days upon weeks!

I would build, dismantle and rebuild it all over again! I would pretend that the Lego police that came with the set only had five minutes to build the chopper before the criminals came down to the water, though it would take me a little longer than that because I had to make dialogue for the characters, and I was hopeless at multitasking back then.

On the 9th of May (four days after I'd turned six) Dad went off to a dental appointment in Hungary. This was something I can't even remember, but I'll try my best to inform you of why.

The simplest and most obvious reason is that... Hungary has better dental care than Britain does!

On the 26th of May, we had an Art Day. Again, I do not see the point in this, and I don't think the school does either because we stopped doing it past Year 4. Like French Day, our class learnt about a particular artist; Vincent Van Gogh. We learnt about his painting called, "Sunflowers". Did you Know that "sunflowers" wasn't just 1 painting? No! Vincent did several paintings of the famous yellow flower.

Also, it is suspected that he cut off his ear in a fit of epilepsy. To add to that, he killed himself because he was either feeling like a millstone around his brother (Theo Van Gogh)'s neck, or he was so mentally unstable that he shot himself in the stomach.

On the penultimate (second last) day of May, we went on a school trip to the London Eye. At first, Elon, Anthony and I were all saying that it would be a walk in the park. Then, when we could see the London Eye, Elon and Anthony were crying, and I said to myself "Welp. This is where we're going to die now. It was nice knowing ya, world!". Obviously, there was nothing to worry about, and I thoroughly enjoyed seeing London from the top of the Eye. Fun times!

The Great Fire of London school play:

On the 23rd, we had a school play. School plays are literally in the name - it's a play hosted by a year group! Our Year 1 play was about the Great Fire of London, and I was Samuel Peeps, the mayor at that time. I love school plays because not only do you skip lessons, but, since year 4, there is supposed to be a band for the play (the children who can play instruments, including myself, make up the people for the band)!

Last week of Year 1:

In the last week of Year 1, some nice things happened. For one, I became an orange belt; yep, I had two gradings in the space of a couple of months. If I had a grading twice a year, every year, I would be a purple belt by know. It would be a black belt if it were not for the fact that you must wait a year before you can be a black belt from a purple belt.

WORDS TAKE SHAPE:

I guess I didn't really explain how the karate system works in terms of belts. There are 12 belts – that is, if you exclude the black belt dans. In order, they are white belt, white belt orange stripe, orange belt, red belt, yellow belt, green belt, blue belt, brown belt white stripe (the belt I currently own), brown belt two white stripe, purple belt, then black belt. Then, there are 10 black belt dans. There are 12 kyus, the twelfth being the white belt and the first being the black belt.

Anyways, this was the third time I'd gotten a C+, which was the third lowest grade you can get. I have only gotten anything higher once, and that was my latest grading, when I got a brown belt white stripe. I didn't really fuss about that back then; all I wanted was to get another belt. The feeling of the crisp new belt compared to your old, worn one is oh so satisfying!

The second thing was the school party. We had so much fun after lunch, which is when all class parties start. We watched the `Willy Wonka` movie on the interactive board and ate lots of delicious party food. We all brought some food into school on that day. I brought in some cupcakes, which everyone immediately wanted to stuff themselves silly with. Miss saw all the hubbub and told me to hand them out.

I had a big brain idea at that moment. I handed them out to the people who didn't rush for them first, then put them away on the table. Making it seem like I had forgotten. Then, I stood back up after a while and very slowly handed them out to the rest of the people. That wasn't the funniest part. The thing that made me want to laugh until my ears went blue and my shoes fell off was that Mrs. Sogi didn't say anything. She saw it all but didn't scold me or even make a comment! Hilarious!

Yes! Words Are Wonderful.

Nothing but Nouns:

Nouns are some of the most basic parts of grammar. They are things, places or people. Pretty simple, right?

You must remember that there are three types of nouns:

- Collective nouns.
- Common nouns.
- Proper nouns.

Common nouns name kinds of things. For example, "the cat ate the rat". Cat and rat are both nouns. A cat is an animal, and so is a rat. They're both things. See? That wasn't too hard!

Then, we have proper nouns. Proper nouns are the name of places or things. "Charlie" is a proper noun because it is a particular person.

Collective nouns name groups of things. You've heard of "a herd of sheep", haven't you? Well, "herd" is a collective noun, because it is a group of sheep. Here's a piece of unnecessary information you will never, ever need! A group of normal fish is a school, but a group of Jellyfish is a smack! K.O!

Pronouns are words that replace nouns. Be careful with them, though.

If you said, "Jackie let her dog off its leash, and she chased the ball around the park", we'd have a problem. You could either mean the dog chased the ball around the park, or that Jackie did, which would be downright weird. You also wouldn't hear "Jackie took Jackie's coat"; it would be, "Jackie took her coat".

Here are some nouns that you can use when you're writing:

Entry level:

- Boy
- Girl
- Dog
- Cat
- Mouse
- Cheese
- Car
- He
- Her

Intermediate level:

- Banana
- Tiger
- Lizard
- They
- Them
- Their
- Blade
- Shield

Mastery level:

- Crustaceans
- Mammals
- Reptiles
- Eiffel Tower
- Statue of Liberty

- Tik Tok
- Among Us
- Herr (the German term for a man)
- Quay (a platform used for loading and unloading cargo boats)
- Quay (pronounced "key". Don't know why, but the English language is strange three-quarters of the time. It means "a platform for unloading and loading ships". That's a queer quay, that is!)

Noun Quiz:

Do you think you have gotten a grasp of nouns?

See how good you really are with my ultimate quiz!

1) What is a collective noun? Is it:

   a) Some gibberish teachers want to force into your brains
   b) A place, person, or thing
   c) A magical potion

   _____

2) Use nouns that are these things:
    a. Food

   _____

Nothing but Nouns:

    b. Man

    _____

    c. Car

    _____

    d. Movie

    _____

    e. Device

    _____

    f. Weapon

    _____

    g. Type of clothing

    _____

3) What does a pronoun do and why do we use them?

_____

_____

Yes! Words Are Wonderful.

Common nouns name things.

ghost   book   snail

Here is the noun test.
Can you put a, an or the in front of it?
✓ It is a common noun. ✗ It is not a common noun.

- Test these words with a, an or the.

_____ ghost	✓	_____ glue	
_____ sit		_____ paper	
a rubbish		_____ sing	
_____ blue		_____ clever	
_____ bike		_____ silly	
_____ curly		_____ corner	
_____ face		_____ brown	
_____ eat		_____ up	

The noun tests

NOW TRY THIS!

- Underline the common nouns.

A lion woke up when a mouse ran over his face. He jumped up and

grabbed the mouse and was about to kill him. The mouse asked the lion to let go and said that one day it could

Did you manage to get through that?

Good, because they don't get any easier as we go along!

Nothing but Nouns:

A New Layer of Words

Once 2017 rolled around, the fine specimen of which I am talking about learnt how to write whole paragraphs, causing a huge evolutionary advancement in my writing. I love the flow of the words as they form a wonderful new story. I also craved finding synonyms (words that mean the same as other words) for words to give my writing that extra bit of pizazz.

A few actual diary entries by DJ in 2017

Friday, 6/1/2017

I was excited about February being on the horizon. T.M joined the school today. T.M later went on to become the most... unique person I know and a great friend. Back then, he formed a bond with us (my friends and I) after playing an intense game of It (tag) at playtime.

Sunday, 8/1/2017

Dad and I went to the park. Whilst there, I went to the skate park and used my scooter there. I was usually far too afraid to use the ramps or anything, sticking to going round and round the little complex of ramps in the middle of the skate park.

Today, however, I mustered up the courage to go on 1 of the dinkiest little ramps there. It was a straight-cut, gentle slope, and I didn't even go down it; I just went across the side of it with the momentum generated by about three dozen laps around the skate park itself. It took me a few attempts to get on the slope from the side of the biggest ramp I'd ever seen to the dinkiest slope in history, but I managed in the end.

Wednesday, 11/1/2017

I went swimming today and I was in Stage Two. My instructor was funny.

Tuesday, 17/1/2017

I did my karate exercises with my Dad this morning. We learnt about synagogues in R.E. There was a new boy in karate.

Wednesday, 1/2/2017

Achieving Stage Three Swimming, sent me soaring over the moon with glee! I mean, who wouldn't be happy if they were moved up a stage after only 2 lessons in the previous 1? This guy certainly would!

Wednesday, 8/2/2017

An Einstein moment just popped into my head. If I can write sentences in the evening, why can't I do that in the morning? This would make writing my sentences much more time efficient… hmmm. My P.E. lesson involved a game of basketball. By the way, P.E. stands for Physical Education.

Yes! Words Are Wonderful.

Thursday, 23/2/2017

I was full of beans in anticipation of swimming. Our instructor taught us how to do the sink push and glide (push and glide underwater).

Monday, 3/4/2017

I was hyped for swimming today. Anything to do with swimming gets me hyperactive... Now that I think about it, pretty much everything can get me to go into overdrive. After about an hour of intense paddling, floating and cavorting, Mum and I went home and had some top-tier oxtail. Or as I like to call it, Beef on Bone.

Saturday, 8/4/2017

Today is the play date with one of my favourite people on Earth, Anthony! He has been my friend since I first joined Selwyn, so no wonder I was excited. First, we went to ODEON to watch the `*B*oss baby`, which was hilarious. The main draft is that there's a boy called Tim Templeton who has a little brother who secretly works in a business run just by babies to increase the "Baby Love" in the world until everyone loves babies and babies only. One day, he takes Tim into his workplace and they have a fun time.

Then, we went back home, and he fell down the stairs. The reason for this was that he and I were trying to be extra-sneaky in the hopes of scaring Mum. He tried to jump down the stairs, tripped over one of them and rolled down the rest of the stairs. Even to this day I can remember how idiotic and funny he was then (he's moved to Berlin now). Sadly, he had to go back home after a while, but it was fun while it lasted! I loved it so much, the next day I kept replaying that day in my mind!

Sunday, 23/4/2017

My cut felt a little better today. Mum put purple dressing on it, and it fought any possible bacteria. I added more depth to my ant farm, which was coming along smoothly. It could almost reach the bottom of my calf now, but a usual ant farm for wild ants can be as deep as a grown man is tall!

Wednesday, 26/4/2017

I tried to do parkour at playtime, which did not work in the slightest *sigh*. I had taken quite a bit of interest in parkour, which looked like so much fun on the YouTube videos, but, obviously, was 10 quintillion times harder doing it.

When I went to swimming, I had a bit of trouble getting out of the pool because I can't really hoist myself up and out of the pool like most of the other kids in my class. Well, I guess that meant I just had to keep going at it, huh?

Yes! Words Are Wonderful.

Friday, 5/5/2017

Today I am overly excited because it is my birthday, and we went to Colchester zoo. Once again, I had 3 of my favourite things put together. Birthdays, zoos and wildlife... though I guess wildlife is included in zoos. Whilst there, we saw the big five.

If you didn't know already, unfortunately, in Africa, the Big Five includes animals that are now some of the most endangered animals on the planet... Rhinos are critically endangered, whereas lions, elephants, and leopards are vulnerable and Cape Buffalo are the least threatened. When we looked at the Ostrich cage, one of the Ostriches snapped at me!

Personally, I was offended. I wanted to see the Ostriches the most and one of them decides to think to itself: "All right, let me just spoil this kid's day. The question is, how? Ooh I know! Just snap at his little juicy fingers!" Probably not, but still! We then went to a restaurant before coming home.

HOLIDAY HOUR!

This marks the time I went on holiday to Jamaica. Believe me, it was barrels of fun!

Wednesday, 26/7/2017

Today I am excited because we are going to beautiful Jamaica, the home country of most of my family. My siblings, aunties and uncles from my Mum's and Dad's sides and quite a few others I probably don't even know exist are from Jamaica, so it's nice to go there.

As we boarded the plane, I felt Trunkie, my unofficially named suitcase-on-wheels (don't ask) shivering because obviously suitcases have a conscience or feelings. When we came for a landing, my ears were popping, and one of the flight attendants told me to blow hard out of my nose whilst pinching it, which HURTS!

Wednesday, 2/8/2017

Today Uncle Denzel drove us to my Auntie Colene's house. Auntie Colene is one of, if not the kindest soul you will ever meet except, of course, God and Jesus, and her cooking rivals that of Mum's and Auntie Marcia's, so I love it when we visit there. The room we were staying in was amazingly comfortable. I used Mum's phone until we went to bed.

Thursday, 3/8/2017

Today we celebrated Mitri's birthday!

Mitri, or as I call her, the DJ clone, thanks to our many quirky similarities, had turned 21, which is still incredibly young, despite everything Kashief says about anything over 20 is elderly.

I was so happy!

Yes! Words Are Wonderful.

Saturday, 19/8/2017

This morning, I decided to have breakfast early. I'm not sure why, it was just something I decided to do. It's just one of those weird decisions that you do with no clue about why you're doing it.

Then Dad came with my suit for the funeral, and I immediately felt the prickling of tears in the back of my eyes. Not only did I not like suits, but Grandma had died! Kashif got me dressed and I felt very posh, although you wouldn't see it because I made such a face that you'd think I either had constipation or that I was being abused by the people who had "forced" me into the "smart-looking straitjacket".

When we got to church, Mum was crying so I cheered her up by telling her that Grandma wouldn't want her to cry, would she? At one point, I cried so hard I thought there would be no more water left inside of me! *Sigh*. So much for consoling Mum. When we got back, I just went straight to bed because, for those of you who do not know, going to funerals and crying until you feel like your eyes have shriveled up to the size of a raisin and fallen out is a very tiring experience.

A New Level of Words Resumed

The Inky Ages:

You might be wondering what on earth the inky ages are. Well, this is when I started my third year of school <u>and </u>when I first got a pen license, which is a certificate you must earn every school year to be able to use a pen. They can and will be taken away from you if your writing starts to look like dog sick though, so keep your good handwriting consistent!

ADVERBS AND ADJECTIVES:

Hey! Do you want to know the secret to making your writing have a little more pizzazz? Well, you've come to the right piece of text! Two words are the key to having explosive writing. Number one: "Adjectives". Adjectives are words that describe things. They describe nouns and give you extra information about them. They just give you a bigger and better picture of what's going on.

For example, "The caterpillar wore socks. It was a long caterpillar." That's a very boring sentence, isn't it? Let's say, "The caterpillar wore baggy, pink socks. It was a massive caterpillar. See? Baggy and pink are both describing the socks, and massive is describing how the caterpillar is a noticeably big, chunky larvae (the name for baby insects).

Adverbs do one thing. - They you guessed it! - add more information to verbs. They usually end in -ly. Imagine you're describing someone walking from school. Let's call him Barry.

You could say, "Barry ran from school", or, you could say "Barry ran swiftly from school". Be careful, though. Words like "lovely" and "friendly" aren't adverbs. They are adjectives. Not all adverbs have to end in -ly to be adverbs. They only need to describe the verb.

Yes! Words Are Wonderful.

Try using these words in your writing and find some synonyms for them:

Entry level:
- Slowly
- Slow
- Quickly
- Quick
- Sleepily
- Tired
- Hungrily
- Hungry
- Thirstily
- Thirsty

Moderate level:
- Sluggishly
- Sluggish
- Rapidly
- Rapid
- Promisingly
- Promising
- Boldly
- Bold
- Barely
- Almost

Mastery level:
- Superiorly
- Superior
- Gallantly

ADVERBS AND ADJECTIVES:

- Gallant
- Deliberately
- Deliberate

Another quiz for you right here!

Try it if you dare…:

1) What do adverbs do?

   _____

2) Write three adverbs describing time and three adjectives to describe a car.

   _____

   _____

   _____

3) Write three adjectives describing a place, time and thing.

   _____

   _____

Yes! Words Are Wonderful.

Words for describing

These words describe someone or something.

tall   round   sad   wavy   long   soft   hot

In sentences they describe nouns.

- Circle the words that describe the nouns.

1 There was a tall green plant growing beside the small cottage.

2 An angry woman was shaking her fist at her young son.

3 The frightened lad began to climb up the enormous plant.

4 "The cow was old. This beanstalk is wonderful," he said.

5 He looked up and saw a pair of huge boots.

6 The huge boots were on a pair of gigantic feet on the ends of two massive legs.

NOW TRY THIS!
- Write two sentences to continue the story.
- Underline the nouns.
- Add a word to describe each noun.

Teachers' note Remind the children of the different purposes of words in a sentence: to name people or things (or to use instead of these names), to show actions, to say where, when or why things happened and to show belonging. Tell them that they are going to investigate words which describe things, people and places. Emphasise that these words describe nouns.

100% New Developing Literacy
Sentence Structure and
Punctuation: Ages 7–8
© A & C BLACK

Actual Diary entries from 2017 – DJ age 7:

Wednesday 23/8/2017

Today Dad and I went to the doctor to get our eyes checked. Turns out, we both had pink eye! We probably got it from Mum, who had to stay back in Jamaica due to her having pink eye. 'We're just a sick family now, aren't we?' I thought to myself as the doctor gave us a prescription for some eye drops.

Different Words Have Similar Meanings:

Saturday 3/9/2017

At what I think was around the 3rd of September, I was over the moon with joy at the fact that today was the first day of karate for year three. It may or may not be, as I am unsure of the exact date! This was overly exciting because this made two things that I enjoy so very much into one day; starting a new year (I was halfway there to year 6!) but I got to do my favourite sport for a whole hour after school!

 When I got to class it was like being in a palace. Everything seemed so big compared to our Year 2 classroom, which was a genuinely nice change! It was almost like we were ants moving into our bigger (and even more carefully constructed, seeing as our school was now a Fancy Dancy `smart` building) nest. In first break, I played The Boy who Cried Wolf. For lunch I had macaroni and cheese. In topic, we designed a shield from ancient times. At karate we did some grading work.

Saturday 12/9/2017

I was so energetic this morning that I almost forgot to get ready for school! At breakfast club, I had a brioche with jam and pretended that I was a Pokémon. Even now, I love pokemon. Not only is it a fun thing to play (and be, in my case), but it expands your imagination to places you would've never thought would be possible in your wildest dreams! This is not a paid promotion but for all parents who have kids over the age of six and are reading this, try it out!

Trust me when I say, my kicking strength has improved greatly since my first karate lesson of Year three. Before, I could barely kick the dummy and leave a half-decently sized indent whereas now, I can kick the dummy with minimum force applied and leave quite a sore stomach for the poor punching bag who foolishly decided to cross me. Hah hah hah!

Sunday 13/9/2017

Today is swimming day (which I love almost as much as my karate lessons), but I had to go without goggles. For those of you lucky souls who have either never had the misfortune of swimming without your goggles or are not fazed by the water touching your eyes, let me tell you that it is painful. It is a lot less painful when you are swimming backstroke because your face isn't in the water or at least, is not supposed to be, anyways, I did a sink push and glide.

Different Words Have Similar Meanings:

Monday 2/10/2017

This morning, I woke up and somehow found myself in Mum's room! I went into super-sleuth DJ mode, and deduced that the only possible explanation was that I sleepwalked into my parents' room. It's not like I just listened to Mum's explanation and copied it almost word for word! No, no, no!

Before I went downstairs, I said an extra-long prayer to God and Jesus {author's note: back then I (yes, I am the specimen!) didn't realise that they were the same person when I wrote this}. At breakfast club, I had toast with some butter and delicious honey! In class, we comprehended a piece of text. For lunch, I had a scrumptious bowl of pasta.

Tuesday 3/10/2017

At 5:30am, I felt someone poke me in the ribs and I realised it was Mum! Well, I can't complain; it is an efficient way to wake a sleeping person up. Fast forward to schooltime, we subtracted using the column method in maths, one of my all-time favourite subjects (aside from English, of course).

After I had my filling meal of a Jacket Potato with cheese (or as the lunch-ladies like to call it, "cheesy parcel surprise") at lunchtime, Anthony and I talked about all the plans we had made for world domination and how we could improve them. You know, classic activities!

Yes! Words Are Wonderful.

Sunday, 7/10/2017

The day had finally come! Today was the day Anthony and I went to the Feel-Good Centre! Firstly, we went to the Feel-Good Centre and I did a massive leap onto the monkey bars whilst Anthony belly flopped into the foam cube pits that he could find; it was a favourite activity of his, apparently.

Then, we went to the park, which was almost as fun as the centre, but not as much. There weren't any monkey bars to try and fail to swing or anything. Finally, we went to Harvester's, where I had chicken strips, Mum had the greasiest burger that I'd ever seen, and Anthony showed his love for fish and chips by asking for the adult version after he'd had the kiddy one! I was so sad when he left.

Sunday 5/8/ 2018

Yahoo! Today is BBQ day! The first over five-year-old kid to come was Krystal then Jayden came along. Of course, a three-year-old came. For entertainment, we played on my Wii; Mario and Sonic at the 2012 Olympics. We then played super Mario Galaxy 2.

Monday morning, I felt a little downhearted because my sister Dimitria didn't come to the BBQ. Why Mitri, Why? Mum was forceful, she said if I wanted my breakfast, I need to fix my face. I was down and did not feel like having breakfast. If Mitri had come I would have been better…

The summer meandered on, today is Tuesday but it was exciting because I was having karate lessons this evening. The final one before September… I can then spend the rest of my summer holidays chillaxing. It should not mean that I stop training, should it?

When I rolled up to the centre just before 4:25pm, dressed in my outfit, I found that there were not many students there. We worked on sharpening our techniques and used cones as markers in the hall. Those students below yellow belts really struggled when we did abs strikes. I found it very enjoyable anyway.

Saturday 11/8/ 2018

I never talk about this much, but today I had a strange coincidence. This was because I did something that made me cry tears of joy, then we went to an exciting event, as if to congratulate me for my efforts because I had cracked it, I am a cyclist… After a while, Mum, Dad and I went to a festival in our community called Chingfest.

I was so surprised; I didn't believe it at first! I am gullible so you must know now why I would be surprised. I cried tears of joy because after much shouting and effort I managed to do eight laps on my bike. I thought Kashief was the best teacher and Dad to be the second best they could both teach me at the same time.

When, Mum and Dad and I went to a festival called Chingfest. The first activity I did was tennis. It creeped me out a bit because it had a lock… A few minutes before we left, guess who we came across… Viv – the lady who works on reception at the karate club. We stood around for a while longer and Dad and I went to find food from a stall. The hotdog he bought me was not great at all; it wasn't hot, and the rain made it even more undesirable.

Yes! Words Are Wonderful.

Thursday 16/08/2018

Guess who came to the house this evening, Raymond! He came with his parents who had come over from UAE; As soon as he came in, he wanted to go outside. We found a snail as soon as we went out; we named it Gary. I soon found another smaller one and named GJ (Gary Junior).

When we came returned inside Raymond felt hungry, so I made us a sandwich each. I gave him a Mickey mouse plate and all I got was an insult....

Friday 17/08/2018

I was saddened because Raymond left England for the UAE the night before. I remembered hearing them talking about packing suitcases. Maybe they were going to suitcase land....

Today was a quiet kind of day. Do you know those days when basically nothing happens? This is one of those days. If I went to the dentist, maybe some flare would occur...

At dinner time I had some chicken dippers and chips. I switched on the telly and watched the Mr. Peabody and Sherman show. It gave me an interview of Cleopatra. Talk about a historical report!

Understanding punctuation and phrases

CONNECTIVES:

There are oodles of different types of connectives that you can use.

CONJUNCTIONS:

A conjunction is a word that joins other words together. They could be because, and, but therefore or also. You could say "Daniel ate his cake first because it looked so good." Because is joining the two clauses together.

PREPOSITION PHRASES:

Preposition phrases show the link between one sentence and the next. They are relationship words. An example is "Dan was unsure of how to read the map. In other words, he was lost."

ADVERBS:

Yes! Our beloved adverbs can be connectives! They could be single words like "suddenly", or word phrases like "At last". An example is "The car had started to burn. Immediately, Dan had second thoughts about taking the dare."

Parentheses:

COLONS:

See? I just used a colon! Colons are most used to indicate the start of a list. The sentence, "For the cake, you will need: A large mango, 250g of grated toenails, a skinny man holding a phone and a toy car with the name 'Zoomy Mc Zoom Face' written on its sides" is a great use of a colon. Not sure why you'll need a skinny man, grated toenails or a toy car with an incredibly stupid name written on it, but at least it tells you all the things you'd need.

Colons can also be used for dividing a sentence in which the second slice describes the first or gives you extra information about it. For example, "The room used for the party had been burnt to little more than a crisp: Gassy Greg had exploded and became the first human stink bomb." They're a little like semi-colons, a phrase I'll explain later.

SEMI COLONS:

Didn't take that long, did it? Semi-colons are used for either morphing two sentences into one or separating items in a list. When morphing sentences, you must never, ever forget to make sure that the sentences mean the same thing. If you said, "The car door burst open; the elite members of the FBI strode quickly into their HQ.", then that would be a brilliant example of a semi-colon and you can go pat yourself on the back or something, I don't know.

BRACKETS:

Brackets are used to separate extra information from the main body of the text. The extra bit of info could be an explanation to a tricky word or an interruption to make it seem like the author just thought of it. They are always used in pairs like this: (blah blah blah rhubarb pie carrot blah blah blah). They go around the extra words and sort of herd them in. Like Literary sheep dogs.

DASHES AND COMMAS:

You can use a comma in the same way you do with brackets, herding the extra information into one little pocket. You could say "Johnnie, the biggest giant of No Man's Land by far, swung his club around his head." The two commas separate the fact that Johnnie was the biggest giant of No Man's Land from everything else, making it an embedded clause.

Dashes can also be substitutes for brackets, although that's just one of their uses. You don't have to use dashes in pairs; you can use them to show a dramatic pause, like saying "John looked in the cupboard and the only thing there was - the black diamond". They can also be used to indicate the start of a list.

Yes! Words Are Wonderful.

Example of Preposition phrases and conjunctions:

Entry level:

- In the deepest recesses of the ocean
- On the perilous cliff
- Across the Yellow Brick Road
- Because he ate the banana
- Since she could remember
- Before he was born

Moderate level:

- Inside the velvety room
- Beside the cavernous classroom
- On top of the flourishing tree

Mastery level:

- In exchange for the goods,
- Because of his disability,
- Once upon a time,
- Fifty thousand millennia ago,
- In the line of sight,
- In retrospect,

Understanding punctuation and phrases

Quiz:

Here is another quiz for you! I've made it even harder than before, so BEWARE!

1)   Which is the correct phrase for this sentence?

      a)   Trust Sharon to have everything .... control.

          i. Throughout control
          ii. Over control
          iii. Under control
          iv. Below control

_____

2)   Write three examples of prepositional connectives and three conjunctions:

      a)   Prepositional:

_____

      b)   Conjunctions:

_____

      c)   The comma store:

_____

Yes! Words Are Wonderful.

The comma store

- **Show the comma keepers where to put commas.**

She bought a loaf two oranges a melon and a bag of sugar.

I counted four sparrows six wagtails twelve swallows and ten bluetits.

At the new leisure centre we can swim play tennis or football and learn judo.

We know how to use full stops question marks exclamation marks and commas.

At the fair there were roundabouts dodgem cars hoopla donkeys and a roller coaster.

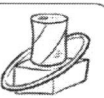

Ants bees wasps flies ladybirds and beetles are all insects.

NOW TRY THIS!
- Write a sentence listing what you did before you set off for school today.

Don't forget the commas.

Teachers' note Remind the children of their previous work on commas in lists and demonstrate how they are useful by reading the first unpunctuated list. Note that the last item in the list has *and* before it and point out that there should be no comma there because *and* is used instead of the last comma.

100% New Developing Literacy
Sentence Structure and
Punctuation: Ages 7–8
© A & C BLACK

Word journey level 5... What a Jive?

Year five had to be the queerest year of school so far. Forget that idea, actually; year 6 takes the cake for that award. You may have not noticed, but we kinda have a deadly virus ravaging the world around us. Anyways, it was a jive of an experience!

A Few actual Diary entries from 2019 – DJ age

Wednesday 25/09/2019

My first thoughts when entering the classroom were "Why on earth can Mr. Barker make a perfect Pingo impression?". Don't ask me where I get the strangest thoughts from; it just sort of... happens. That was because the first thing I heard when I came into the class was a Pingo sounding teacher. I know, strange, right?

At after school club, I had a massive problem. And that problem was girls. They kept following me around everywhere - apart from the little boys' room - and it was almost depressing. To solve my problem, I went home. Only joking! I did a spinning flip off the monkey bars and was called unhuman.

Saturday 28/09/2019

Today it was Mum's birthday, so I made a little surprise for her. Her first surprise waiting for her was breakfast in bed. The second surprise (the one I forgot to show her) was a drawing of her, Dad and me. I was excited because it was Carol's 50th birthday (which she called her forty tenth). My imaginary friend, Bill, congratulated me.

Almost malevolently, the Boom Blaster Dad brought home disobeyed him by refusing to connect to the TV. He thought it played its song with the tone of that of a truck; Dad was unimpressed with its failure to connect to the TV. And trust me when I say that Dad has been disappointed with many gadgets before.

Mum and Dad had arranged for Dad to be Mum's chauffeur. Therefore, Dad drove us to Auntie Carol's birthday party. I watched part of Britain's Got Talent at the house but soon felt groggy and knew it was time to go home.

Monday 7/10/2019

I woke to the uncomfortable scratching on my arm. I ignored it but only because I was watching the time. Before I went to bed last night, it was decided by Dad that I was now forbidden to do my exercises downstairs, as he didn't trust that I have been doing my push-ups without his watchful eyes rooting me out. That didn't bother me much because I wanted him to see my work.

After what happened in the classroom today, I felt that there was an eerie chill aimed directly at me. What had happened was that I was doing my test like everyone else. There were only 44 questions (kinda the same as year 4), and we had a whopping full hour to do them! I had finished in the first half hour and then when Mr. Barker saw me not doing my work, he just stared at me. Suddenly, I had all eyes fixed icily on me.

Friday 11/10/2019

Do you know when people say that eating cheese before bed gives you nightmares? Well, imagine you had that nightmare but 100 times funnier, and that's the dream I had last night. It was very gory, but it was as hilarious as a clown with a contagious laugh. I was splattered with blood from a ketchup monster (please, just don't ask).

In PSHE, we had a debate about Brexit. Kacey, Yak, and I were the pupils to debate with years 5 and 6 pupils. Unluckily for me, I wasn't one of the six pupils chosen to participate in a debate against our partner school, Davies Lane. I wasn't too bothered because I did it in year 4.

It got more enticing and funnier when Mr. Barker told us to do multiplication without writing any numbers at all. It's complicated to explain in words, but if I had a sheet of paper, I could do the primary times table without writing a word or sign. If you don't believe me, I understand because I didn't at first either. I was kinda like, "Is this me or am I still asleep in bed and had I just dreamed all of what happened so far?

Wednesday 16/10/2019

Having jumped up and realised the time I nearly exploded with excitement. "Mind where you are going, D.J.!" Musu, my imaginary pet dragon exclaimed. "I have feelings!" "Sorry Musu", I said, "Just really excited". If you think that imaginary friends are for babies, well you're well wrong. I have one, and he's fantastic!

when I got to school, we had to write in the perspective of Stella-Artois (Michael's dog) for our short write. It wasn't that hard for me because I had read the book before and listened to Stella's side of the story; I imagined how the dog felt.

The afterschool club was on us again. I found a ginormous horde of mushrooms and told Miss Bridgette. We were all evacuated from the playground because she had encountered these mushrooms before. They were poisonous mushrooms according to her; I could tell even without my wildlife book that these were edible mushrooms. They were only a harmless bunch of chicken of the woods (laetiporus sulphuerus)

Friday 18/10/2019

This morning, I was delighted at the fact that today was the last day of school. What I was not happy with was the fact that I had a nasty lump on my head. After a delicious breakfast and a soothing ice cube, I was ready for the day.

Everyone in the class loved our science lesson as it involved Oreos – lots and lots of Oreos. All we had to do was show the 8 phases of the moon as partners – kind of like a school project. Tommy and I drew circles, put the Oreos in it, and cut off the parts of the cream to show the different phases.

As if my day couldn't get any more exciting, I went to Keion's house! Keion showed me his new room (including a bunk bed), and then we played on his Xbox. We had pizza for dinner, but right after, I went home. That didn't dampen my spirit.

Word journey level 5... What a Jive?

Thursday 31/10/2019

Happy Halloween! This ghoulish morning, I woke up with a degree of festivity flowing through me. Everyone else must have had a similar feeling because I had heard many people shouting, "Happy Halloween!" out of their windows. My Mum and Dad were not among them; they didn't seem very cheery this morning. It is the birthday of the devil, after all.

Ellie and I had a friendly match of tennis at acorn club. Instead of playing it in the air, we pushed the ball on the floor. There were no points, and we didn't have to search about on the hills for the ball if either of us hit it too hard. Overall, it was a win/win!

Swimming lesson came around quickly; I had to practise climbing out of the pool without a ladder. When I tried by the deep end, I gained lots of cramps and nearly threw up (100% exaggeration right there, folks). In the shallow end, I had cramps as well but managed to climb out without help...

Friday 1/11/2019

I woke up late this morning; so much so that by the time I was going downstairs to have my breakfast, it was 14 to 7! This worried me deeply because these days, I am determined to get to school on time. Luckily, I got to the school gates at 7:30am. It was all thanks to Dad, who kept his cool even when I was freaking out.

Elon was disappointed that we had the highest attendance this week because that meant Mulberry class had the climbing frame for the day. He wanted to play freeze tag, but we were on the climbing frame, so he thought that was the end for his freeze tag idea once we got there. Once he saw us playing on it (the climbing frame), though, he completely changed his mind.

I thought Mum was going to pick me up from after school club but, boy; was I wrong. She had parked her car in front of the school, gates which used to be illegal, so she could be the first person to pick me up instantly. We had to go on a shopping trip, and I met lots of children from my year, including Yak, Alexa, and Tara.

Monday 4/11/2019

I had gotten out of bed extra early today so that I could start my story. It also meant I had to remain extra quiet in order not to wake my parents up. "Smack! Smack! Smack!" my flip flops were making a racket. Then, as if the universe decided that it wanted to have a laugh, I tripped over one of the stairs and fell backwards. BOOOOSH! Had they woken up? No, good. I was now a ninja, moving sneakily in and out of the shadows until I reached the door into their room. Gently, I opened it, let myself in and proceeded to do my stretching.

Our class had the climbing frame and football cage today! Only Mulberry class today... It was made even better when Henry, Max, and Yak were not allowed to set foot anywhere near it. This seemed to be accurate, and it proved that way. Tommy had a mishap, and Junaid had hurt his toe on the climbing frame; he shouted "Jesus Christ!" Tommy walked up to him and said "No, you mean Jesus F#**!! The Teaching Assistant on duty overheard him, and we all missed the remainder of our playtime and were banned from the cage and climbing frame for three weeks. Elon, Anthony, and I all said to Tommy "you have a serious potty mouth, don't you?!".

The day got worse; we had to tidy up after everyone else at the after-school club. That popped itself to the top of my list of unfortunate events. Then it went to the top of the list of events caused by karma because the people who tidied up could go outside and those who didn't have to go back to the snack line. Unfortunately, I wasn't there to see the humiliation on their faces, but I could well imagine, and my friends would tell in the morning.

Saturday 9/11/2019

Today was one of those days when you forget something awesome is happening and when you remember, you treat as if it was the first piece of good news you've heard in your life. I was just doing my normal Saturday routine when out of the blue, Mum asked me what I was planning to wear for the fireworks event. That is when it all came back to me...

The trip to Dad's school (Mill Hill Foundation) where the fireworks set was very ordinary, took a while. What was awesome, though, was the wait for the school to open. Dad had pushed the car seats back so far; it was as if we were in beds. He said that was what they were designed to do...

When the school opened, the first thing you saw was what looked like a University. Of course, it wasn't. It was instead a boarding school on a vast campus. This wasn't just any old boarding school; it was very luxurious. When the fireworks were set, a child had hurled his glow stick onto the fireworks. That a firework was going to put the words MILL HILL on the sky but instead... well, let's say we got a very neon shower.

Yes! Words Are Wonderful.

Sunday 1/12/2019

December already! How time flies! I thought this morning that it was December tenth, clearly implying that I needed more sleep. Unsurprisingly, when I reminded Mum that we were going to go to squad training for the 5th time; she decided to go shopping to kill time. That, reader, was the start of a long, long shopping spree.

T.K. Maxx was full of foul-smelling oil and soothing body moisture, which had disturbing ingredients in them, right where the shopping spree was held. My only interest was in the thought of squad training and daydreaming (Just so you know, daydreaming only happens to sad people). Many people love to daydream, and some of those people are politicians.

Squad training was a new thing for me; I felt a little out of place.

Tuesday 10/12/2019

Only 15 sleeps till Santa! all the people in breakfast club were feeling the Christmas Vibe and people were wearing jumpers when Christmas jumper day was on Friday. Maxx, who wasn't incredibly happy, was one of the people who were feeling it in their blood – the two ultimate items that are Christmas-related... A Red Rudolph nose and reindeer antlers. Mrs. McGee had to take the antlers off him because he was messing around with them... Epic fail!

Tuesday 17/12/2019

The concert is today! My Rocksteady concert was happening, and even though it meant I had to miss out on P.E., it was worth it. It was good to have my Mum there (that I will explain late)r. First things first, my friends were all happy for me, and Mr. K. made an impression of me playing the guitar.

My maths lesson today was easy; that may be because it was multiplication which is one of my strong points. That said, I got stuck on the last question, and that seemed to deter the others from attempting it since I find multiplication easy-peasy. Even Ms. Shanez was confused!

With rehearsal being a priority for the concert, I left the class-room at 14:00hrs and returned at the end of the school day. When the show was in session, I was propelled by the sight of my Mum in the audience. I played every chord with extreme accuracy and was in perfect time with the two other guitarists in our group. All in; all boring. No guitar riffs with any nice speed or anything!

Wednesday 25/12/ 2019

Christmas day is here!!! I was greeted with a fantastic day, and the following unfolded:

This morning I was the first one up and stirring in the house, itching to open my many presents. Only I was downstairs; Mum had set up late as she always does on these days. I am awake and `full of beans`. Heck, not even a mouse up was up but from me. The morning was eerily quiet. I wrote a poem: …

Yes! Words Are Wonderful.

This poem I thought, would get published as a worse seller. If you're too full of laughter now because of my ramblings, I warn you that people might think you're not right in the head when you're reading this poem. I got to open one present and it was before breakfast, mind you. It was... a bunch of books! I had run out of some to read.

After a very scrumptious meal consisting of all the trimmings, I thought to myself "it was either God has blessed me this Christmas or I had a lot of very loving relatives. Oh! I forgot it was both!" Mum, Dad and I were all wearing matching elf T-shirts; one of Mum's initiatives sitting under the tree opening presents. I was spoilt by the number of gifts I got this year; I will only mention a few of my favourites:

- Mitri had gotten me a lot of clothes, but the sketchpad was the best.
- Mum had gotten me a knitted Poke'mon ball and Pikachu.
- Mum had given me two video games; yeah!!

Sunday, 29/12/ 2019

I thought Today would be a good day starting from the point when Dad found the antenna for my Wii. It meant that the Wii would start responding so I could play video games. I still had my Nintendo 3DS, but that was unfortunately broken, so I could not use it. I started to put my game disc on the Wii when I heard that Raymond is coming to visit.

If you have heard about my cousin Raymond, you will know that he is very hyperactive. For instance, I was playing pokemon battle revolution, and every time I landed a hit, he would shout "yes!". At dinner, we had a plethora of food. Later, the subject of the evening turned to anacondas. According to Raymond, the only way to escape from one is to throw a gerbil at it. After a while, I picked up my sketchpad and started to sketch and, of course, Raymond wanted in on the action. However, he could not sketch from memory. So, Mum said Raymond could pick a pokemon to draw and I find the image on her phone. He wanted to draw a pokemon poster, and he was great at it. What was bad was that he said he was terrible at it. He was great for a beginner!

New Year's Day 2020

Happy New Year!!!!

It's the first day of a new decade; my second decade. It was looking bright and festive on the outside but believed me; I was feeling neither bright nor cheerful... I was pumped up for the new year but something in my heart of hearts told things were not good. Lucky neither of my parents asked if I was okay so I felt safe with my thoughts. Breakfast looked and tasted delicious; Mum had come through again!!

I couldn't eat much to my disappointment because my stomach ached badly. The secret was now out, and my Dad gave me some warm peppermint to drink and put a mouldy lemon on his plate at the same time. I asked if it was poisonous and that led to a whole conversation about pioneers of medicine and medical history. One of these pioneers was Ignaz Semmelweis; he was a person who persuaded early doctors to wash their hands when operating.

Proper hygiene was absent from early medical practice, no wonder survival rates were so low. There is a host of books on the history of medicine. Dad had brought one home from his school for me, I think there is might be something written on the persuasion caused by Ignaz.

Have you ever been in a situation where you are sitting at the dining table with your parents and suddenly your interesting topic spins into songs that you like? Well, that happened to me today, so if it has happened to you, I feel your awkwardness in the moment. Dad asked what my favourite songs were and five minutes later I was stressed out trying to remember a Rag'n'Bone Man song, not sure what to do or say...

January tailed off with a lot of news on LBC about the Coronavirus that was causing a pandemic in the world. I woke up and heard they were calling the disease Covid-19 which Dad explained meant Corona Virus Disease 2019 (the year in which it was discovered in Wuhan, China). I had a slow, rough day even though it was maths day, and you know how I love my maths. We had to redraw our board games three times in a row before we did the final thing.

We also learnt about Pythagoras theorem. In a right-angle angled triangle, $a^2 + b^2 = c^2$; no matter how big or small it is. Guess what nationality Pythagoras was? Do not look it up... Did you? Okay he was indeed Greek.

When I went outside at lunchtime, Colin and I had a parkour showdown, an agility competition. We were judged by Imani and Joshua – the parkour legends of our year. Everyone thought Colin was going to win when he did 360 degrees off the lowest part of the climbing frame. Trust me it's hard, but when I back flipped (more like back flopped) off the shakiest, highest part, the deal was sealed.

The day returned to normal speed when I got back outside and went to Acorn afterschool club...

Then, we got a good ol' dose of lockdown. On the sixteenth of March, Mr. Matt Hancock, health secretary of the UK, pretty much said that we had to stay away from people as much as possible. An anti-socialist's dream. I was fine with it at first, but it would be even better if I were an anti-socialist because then I would be forced to do what my life's dream was. Either way, I was fine for the first week or so.

The school gave us a big swathe of comprehension and maths work to do, which looked about as exciting as getting a vomiting bug. I guess it was for people who could not get any other work. However, as you already know, both of my parents are teachers, so it wasn't like I could fall behind on schoolwork anyways. Not only would I get the primary schooling from the work sheets and Mum, but I would also get some Secondary-level science like Chemistry, Physics and Biology from Dad! That was fine by me - especially the secondary part - because I liked learning anyways.

There was also the idea of our fitness to tackle. Without a doubt, I was the fittest I've ever been, during the lockdown. Sensei Tyrone started to hold karate lessons on zoom, then in the park, before going back on zoom a couple of lessons afterwards. Dad and I went on jogs to the Rugby Pitch near us, (I'm calling it RP), did some exercises that I had done at my karate sessions along with some exercises Dad made up, like explosive squats and push-ups on the tyres that were dotted around the pitch.

Every time we came back home, we'd be pouring with sweat, hungry and tired. It was great exercise, not only for our bodies, but for our minds too! I also did some walking with Mum for a while in the early mornings, which, after a couple of days, turned into doing T25; a 25-minute workout CD that Mum had stashed on the shelf. By the time a few weeks had gone by, I was as fit as a fiddle! Dad taught me all these special tech-

Yes! Words Are Wonderful.

niques like sucking in my stomach and to breathe in very deep when running. We also made some cycling trips to different places, which was also lots of fun. The pedalling was hard, hard work at times, but never really burned that many calories. We went to a section of Epping forest once, and saw lots of things, like some coots in the huge expanse of lake that made that part of Epping forest so enjoyable, a Mallard's NEST which is an all-time first Mallard nest find for me, or any nest for any animal, some frogspawn, dragonflies and much more besides!

Making the best out of being at home all day, Mum decided to take up baking as a hobby. At first, it was nothing complex, just chocolate and sponge cakes. Then, she started making brownies, upside down pineapple cakes, strawberry cakes and much, much more. And she didn't just bake confectioneries; no! She baked bread treats like dinner rolls!

Finally, after 3 months of almost complete solitude, we were told that we could come back to school in June! We were put into random classes with children in our year. My class consisted of Thomas, Elon, Arthur, Alwin, Daniel, Imani, Joshua, Tommy and about two other people including Mrs. Bigrade, our teacher. It was a great class, even if only three people from my class were there. We had the playground split into different `bubbles`; a new form of social distancing.

Our class were in the football cage; we were not allowed to play football until lunchtime break, though. We didn't need some air-filled sphere to entertain ourselves. No sir! We just played bulldog, a game in which someone is the bulldog, and everyone else must run to the other end of wherever they may be playing without getting touched by the bulldog. If you manage to get yourself caught like the slowcoach you may be, which most of the children in my new class were, anyways, you become a bulldog as well. The last person to be caught wins, and then they become bulldog. We had the end of Year 5, where we watched a movie called *'The Peanuts Movie'* and cut out silhouettes of soldiers and planes to go up on our year 6 walls. I came home on that day feeling better than I usually do after finishing a school year. There was only one year left of Selwyn before I was in secondary school! Trust me, you do not know how happy I was feeling on that day!

IDIOMS, NOT IDIOTS!

Have you ever heard someone say, "are you feeling a bit under the weather?" and wonder how on earth people can be below weather? Well, it's an idiom! An idiom cannot be used if you look at it literally; no one is small enough or naturally flexible enough to be wrapped around someone's little finger! (the phrase "wrapped around her little finger"). The thing is, no one can understand an idiom if they can't look at things from any other perspective than that of the logical one.

Then, we have proverbs. They're little sayings that could be anything from, `Too many cooks spoil the broth` to `Don't count your chickens before they hatch`. They could sound like they mean one thing, but they would be changed to be applied to life.

Finally, we have cliches which is pronounced clee-shay. Cliches are overused phrases; fine for talking, but not so much for when you're writing. Try and come up with something a bit more original. Examples are `at the end of the day` (most people commentating on a sports game will say that), `there has to be a level playing field` (important politicians and people commentating on those important people say that a lot!) and `nerves of steel` (you're, really, tough.)

Yes! Words Are Wonderful.

Entry level:

- To go down in flames (to fail spectacularly)
- Cats got your tongue? (you can't speak?)
- Once in a blue moon (exceptionally rarely)
- Down in the dumps (upset)

Intermediate level:

- Make-or-break
- Took its toll (played a part)
- Missed the point
- Turned a blind eye (ignored)

Mastery level:

- Forged ahead
- Pays peanuts
- Raining cats and dogs
- Cool as a cucumber (my personal favorite!)

QUIZ TIME!

Try getting through these tough questions. Don't say I didn't warn you!

1) What does "pays peanuts" mean?

_____

_____

Word journey level 5... What a Jive?

2) Use the idiom "cool as a cucumber" in a sentence.

_____

_____

3) In which kind of text can the phrase "raining cats and dogs" be used literally?

_____

_____

Got it?

Good for you!

ACRONYMS AND MNEMONICS!

Acronyms are made from the first letters of words. Laser is an acronym for (hold on, I am taking the very deepest of breaths...) Light Amplification by Stimulated Emission of Radiation. Phew! I don't know about you people, but I would prefer sticking to a simple `laser`. NASA is an acronym for National Aeronautics and Space Administration. See? It makes life a whole lot easier.

Mnemonics, pronounced Nem-onics, are ridiculous sentences used to help you remember tricky spellings or phrases. A mnemonic for remembering the order of North, East, South and West is Never Eat Shredded Wheat, or Naughty Elephants Squirt Water.

It's fun to make up your own mnemonics; I used to make songs out of times tables. Imagine singing "8 x 4 is 32, 32, 32! 8 x 4 is 32, and you know that's true!" to the tune of Mary had a little lamb (100% not from one of my *Diary of a Wimpy Kid* books), and you'll understand where I'm coming from. The point is, Acronyms and Mnemonics aren't demonic (Sorry. I had to say that.)!

Entry level:

- North East South West (NESW) (Never Eat Shredded Wheat)
- BTW (By the Way)
- FYI (For Your Information)
- LOL (Laugh Out Loud)

ACRONYMS AND MNEMONICS!

Intermediate level:

- Gave me a hand
- Loner
- Bad egg
- Took the words right out of my mouth

Mastery level:

- Wet behind the ears
- Finish with flying colours
- Know… inside out
- Whet my appetite

Quiz time:

1) Why do cliches sound bad when writing?

   _____

2) What does the underlined phrase mean?

   _____

The dogs watched helplessly as the dragons ran riot.

3) Use your three favourite idioms in one sentence.

   _____

Nice work getting through all these toughies!

Only one quiz left!

Yes! Words Are Wonderful.

Words are Communication Tools:

A few actual Diary entries from 2020

September 2020 – year six is here and Corona with it

Tuesday 18/8/ 2020

I was overly excited today.

"What could have possibly made you more excited than you are already?" You may be thinking to yourself "It would have to be something really big". Yes, yes it was. This big news was that Elon's mother has so very kindly invited me over to her house for four hours in a few days' time. That would make anyone who has friends hyped up but there is even more to the story. This would be not only the second time I would be going to Elon's house; t was the first time I would see him in the flesh as a ten-year-old. It was brilliant, outstanding, and purely amazing!

Instead of Mum watching me swim today, she joined me in the pool I was so chuffed! After I swam 30 laps on my part and Mum did 20 laps, we had multiple contests like "who can swim the furthest in the pool without coming up for breath" and "who can push and glide the longest length of the pool". Overall, it was the best fun I have had in ages!

This is the day the heavens opened. This morning, I honed my verbal reasoning skills further. According to Mum, the school she had registered me for had an 11+ exams which didn't involve non-verbal reasoning, so all I need to work on for reasoning was of the verbal kind the test was a cakewalk. When I compare this with the other tests I have done up to now, it was like a university student doing year 2 SATs that were set on easy difficulty. In fact, the only question I got wrong was the last challenge question!

Once Mum and I arrived home, we started preparing dinner. We originally intended to have lasagne but considering how few lasagne sheets we had, we switched our idea to pasta and mince instead. I, as the budding chef I am, grated the cheese and taste tested the dish before it went into the oven. Mum, being the master chef and the adult she is, did all the rest. I know, we make a great team.

Thursday 20/8/2020

Instead of doing my exercise upstairs like I normally would, I carried it out downstairs. The prime reason for this was not that it was much easier to do so before carrying out the plans for the rest of my day. The main reason I did my exercise downstairs was that… I was still under the assumption that we still had the rug in the living room. My brain was half-asleep, OK?

The weather today was beautiful! No joke, there wasn't a cloud in sight and the sun was blasting heat waves down on us. I was reading and having some fruit salad outside in the shade and even then, it was ridiculously hot! My last hope was that the pool would cool me down.

Well, it turns out that today the pool was different; it was lukewarm. This was a let-down for me because I was looking forward to a nice refreshing dip, instead of a plain dip in the pool. I did have lots of fun though! I did a triple flip and then a genuine handstand for 5 seconds and I had Mum pull me around as I floated!

Friday morning rolled around; I was left mostly to my own devices. Once I had my breakfast, my mother went to the shops with Auntie Marcia and a short while later, Dad came downstairs and went up again to start his full day of teaching. I just read and read; the book was called *Good night Mr. Tom*. It is about a deluded old man call Tom Oakley who takes in a sickly, spindly, bruise-covered little boy called William Beech. It's a hair-raising tale.

Boy was it windy! The weather outside was no cool, refreshing Zephyr... This was big boy, gale force wind! When Mum and I sprayed the shopping bags down and put them out to dry, we did not need to leave them there for long as the wind was intense, they were sorted in no time. This high-speed wind threatened Mum's plants.

You know the drill; today at 3:30pm, I had my karate lesson with the squad in the memorial park. We did lots of things like using a skipping technique before running to a not-so nearby cone and running back to the same spot. We were having a sort of hierarchy of who wants to work the hardest. When I came out on top and Malika giving everyone a sweat due to her birthday being yesterday. Good stuff.

Saturday

Has anyone ever woken up feeling like anything and everything could get you ticked off or mad? Yeah... I was that person today. Until I had my breakfast, I was that guy. Once I had swallowed some food and my stomach was full; I was happily

Words are Communication Tools:

reading my book in which Will was called away from Mr. Tom by his mother before being sent to the hospital.

As 10:00am dawned upon us, I started ticking off my Saturday chores one by one. I vacuumed my room, the spare room, the passage, my bathroom, brushed down both sets of stairs; wiped the floors, chest of drawers and windowsills in my own room. I then cleaned my shower and took a shower. Yeah, just some average chores for this awesome 10-year-old!

Today was the day. I felt the true wrath of the electric flyswatter Dad brought home; I respectfully call it the fly fryer. It played out like this: Mum and I were chasing flies out of the house, using our secret weapon as some much-deserved backup. As I lunged out for a fly, I somehow took it out (the winged pest) but got my finger in on the action! Ever since I realised how dangerous humans are to flies in a whole new way.

I took a whole new approach to my life this morning. The first thing I did after waking up was to make up my bed properly. Usually, I would just throw my cover on the bed once I get out of it. Afterwards I brushed my teeth and went upstairs and did my exercises that I had not done for a while. Once the first phase of my day passed, I typed for an hour. A meal of cereal later and did the penultimate test paper in one of the books Mum had given me. Until Mum came downstairs, I read.

Around 1:50pm I finally arrived at my guitar lesson where I was confronted by someone... new. This person was no other than that head teacher of the music academy. Not only that but as we worked through the book, he taught me how to play closed strings without looking at the fretboard, how to keep my notes crisp and sharp and much more... That was topped off by being praised; awesome! I know!

I returned home and Mum and I drove to the swimming pool at Banatynnes health club. On our way we saw a cornucopia of motorcyclists all revving their engines and showing off in the street. In fact, one of them did a wheelie down the road doing at least 60 miles per hour. Once we got to the pool, I did my 20 laps and then tried creating my own stroke I am calling the "Mudfish". It is essentially a breaststroke but without any arm movements. Don't ask, ok?

Tuesday

This morning I completed a chunk of work, exercise, kata and practise papers. Non-verbal reasoning and some maths from books provided by mother were used. I then took a break for a while. Once Mum - who had only recently come from upstairs - had finished watching "Couple's Come Dine with Me", I completed section A of a maths test that Mum had found online. I managed quite well. There were a few questions that I tripped up on by adding unnecessary information.

As the day wore on - which it did at a painfully slowly pace - I read an old favourite called `There's a Boy in the Girls' Bathroom`. It's a strange title, I know, but it covers some deep topics; the main one is to show just how hard it is to believe in oneself. It is about a boy called Bradley, who everyone treats as a monster. Soon he was believing he was a monster himself.

Things start to change when the school counsellor arrives. I won't spoil it, but Bradley goes on the best kind of character arc, eventually being invited to his first birthday since he was in the 3rd Grade!

Even though Mum and I spent 15 minutes longer than we usually do at the pool, I did four widths of it and it knocked the stuffing out of me; so much so that I spent most of the time floating around.

Words are Communication Tools:

I had a long deep think about how I behaved yesterday, Dad had pulled me up because I tried to sneak out of my room without finishing off my journal. I feel bad when I see the hurt, I cause my parents when I lie.

Wednesday came and I had one thing on my mind and that was getting through until 2pm. This was made so much easier by the fact that Mum was shredding paper and I found it interesting. The very thought of seeing the paper being ripped into strips makes me sigh with anticipation. Whist we shredded, we watched "Border Patrol", in this episode it showed people who tried to smuggle packs of illegal cigarettes in a monopoly game, hide more cocaine in what was declared as glassware and much, much more.

When the moment of truth came, I could barely contain myself. Mum and I bought some balloons and two birthday cards for Elon and Zach because that is always a nice thing to do. When I got there, Elon kept attacking Zach in waves with the light up darksabre he got on his actual birth date. Nieve was very distracting but when we played on the Xbox, she showed that she was just as talented as Zach, Elon and I. Yeah! Just the norm in Elon's house!

Here's a nice piece of advice I am going to give you from firsthand experience. Never and I mean never, have spicy prawns and fried rice after some pizza and curry fries. My God will your stomach ache afterwards. How do I know this? Well, I already told you – I got a hard dose of experience this evening.

Thursday 27/8/2020

What a good night's sleep I had! I was so worn-out last evening that I just brought the lids down and camped out in the front room last night. I brought my alarm clock down, but I knew that Mum would kill me if I woke her up, so I turned it down to its minimum volume. What I failed to realise was that the alarm wouldn't wake me up if it didn't wake up Mum, At least I got in a great deal more sleep.

Being hard working, I quickly finished my maths test and moved on to the non-verbal reasoning. On reflection I performed much better in my non-verbal reasoning than in my maths. Then again, my brain was working so slowly that it recognised shapes better than numbers.

Today's swimming session can only just be put into words to describe it. Well, that may be exaggerating just a little bit. For the first time in literally years, I used the flat board Mum had bought me. At first, I tried using it as a paddle board, which failed horribly. Undaunted, I decided to use it as a jet. I held the float out in front of me and kicked, which was made easier by the board cutting through the water.

The next morning, I had a better attitude towards yesterday's events. I had some crazy dreams about the paddle float being motor-powered; don't ask, this is how my dreams usually unfold. After I had woken up, I completed some dates from my journal on the computer, messed around on the internet and then had some fruit. I decided I would have my actual breakfast later. Once Mum had left, I completed another two sections of my non-verbal reasoning. I strummed a few strings on my guitar and played a few songs from my workbook before settling down with my new book called *The Other Side of Truth.*

As the day progressed, I felt excited as I delved deeper into my book. The main concept of the book is that two children Fenmi and Sade (pronounced Shar-day with a stress on the second syllable) are sent to London after their father is targeted for reporting on the African wrath in his newspaper. The two refugees must tell lie after lie until, at one point, their father is sent to prison in London. With the help of a news reporter, their lives returned to normal, or at least that's what they thought.

At my karate lesson, I witnessed a man have a physically continuous spasm, otherwise known as a fit. In the beginning Sensei Tyrone tried to help the man back on to his wheelchair, but a passerby on the phone with the ambulance said not to. At the end of the lesson, we found out that the man was on medication, drugs, alcohol and that he was disabled.

Saturday

Early to bed, early to rise… I woke up this morning twenty minutes earlier than normal, before my alarm went off. It left me feeling half-asleep as I staggered down the stairs. When I had gained my well-needed energy from my delicious breakfast, my plan for the remainder of the morning unfolded. After a session of transcribing my journal, I would finish off a non-verbal reasoning paper, take a break, then play some tunes on my guitar and watch `Border Patrol`.

Yeah… I did have a noticeably clearer image of my morning but not so much anytime past that. I did watch some *Border Patrol* but got tired and fell asleep mid-episode. When I had woken up again, which took a while, I had my lunch without realising once that I was in pyjamas. A warm shower later and I was back downstairs watching some extreme weather on TV. The programme was called *Britain's Most Extreme Weather.* Man, you would never guess what the show was about from the name, would you?

I have watched the movie, I have also read the book; today, I started the audiobook `White Fang`, one of the best audiobooks of all time (according to both my judgement and the verdict of the millions of people who also use Audible!!). It is about a pup who also uses multiple phases of being a Michael Morpurgo book, *Born to Run*. Trust me, you can never get enough of it.

Only one more day until I am in year six... September is around the corner. Now you may be wondering "alrighty then, DJ you are going to start a new school year. What's so exciting about that?" Well mister or Mrs.; It is so hard to get excited about anything, my next school year will be my last in primary school. Yes, your little bean is growing up! For those of you who think going into a new year in the middle of a pandemic is hard, you're partly right.

Due to my Mum being a good human being and the laws of fair exchange somehow applying here, both of us went to Auntie Marcia's house to give her a pineapple upside down cake for a piece of fish and some oxtail. This meat will be playing an important role in our dinner – it was all mine. Oh, how I longed for dinnertime to arrive!!

Much to my advantage, Allan video-called me later in the day. "Great!", I thought. I mused to myself the best way to pass time. It turns out, Allan was pretty nervous about moving up to year six, the big boy year. After I had reassured him, his passion for *Star Wars* kicked in and he lectured me on *Star Wars*, which was surprisingly fascinating.

Monday 31/8/2020

This morning Dad got his friend Bro Garnet to come around and change the taps in my bathroom. The face basin got new ones and the hot water tap in the bath was secured. All my taps were good to go now and there was no fiddling around especially in the bath. I think the plumber deserved a good paycheck.

At 1:45pm Dad and I set off for my music lesson. Whilst there, I learnt not one, not two, not three but four techniques. I learnt: three new strings; E-minor; A-minor and G-minor; I learnt how to recognise the transition from playing the guitar with my index and middle fingers to playing with my thumb on sheet music, and the four kinds of timings in a piece of music. Not only that but I have almost completed the song book! Amazing!

Later in the day, just like I told him I would, I continued my chat with Allan. After he finished describing what had happened in the last `Star Wars` movie, he proceeded to read a story he had been working on. It was about a young man called Edmund who is in a constant frenzy for all the power in the world. He has not finished it yet, but it was still epic!

Tuesday 1/9/2020

I went back to school as a year six boy, full of beans and the tallest in the school... I was bursting with excitement.

 I felt like I had a little less control of my body, you could say. What I found annoying was the fact that my hands felt as if they had received a good dose of frostbite. Not even that; I felt as if I had almost gone diplegic in my hands! Nothing I tried worked at first. Hot water, rubbing them together, blowing on them, even working them out was a failed attempt. Finally, it hit me... The reason my hands felt paralyzed was that I had kept them in one place. I practically did not move any part of my body for nine hours. I had cold hands, so to speak.

Yes! Words Are Wonderful.

If you saw the scene in my house at around 11:15am, you would have thought; "what a nice family moment!". Yes, I was playing a song in my song book called "Oh when the saints". I had played it once, and Dad then recognised the song. Mum also recognised it but weirdly they both got completely different recognitions. Dad said it was "Oh when the saints" which was right and Mum said it was "Twinkle, twinkle little star". Ah yes, getting the songs mixed up always hit that soft spot in the heart; I agree.

Lunch time rolled around and we had tuna sandwiches. Later Mum and I went off to the swimming pool. I would say that the pool was a thousand times colder than usual, but let's stick to the fact that if the pool's temperature were measured by how nice it was to someone, people would say that its heart was made of stone.

After jumping around in the pool for ten minutes to try and get warm, some men came into the pool and moved in a way that can only be described as thrashing. One slapped the water with his open hands; I called him the slapper. The other kicked his legs so hard you'd think he was trying to burst a steel house down. I called him the kicker. The noise they made combined with the rowdy nature of the children using the pool at that point, was enough to make us leave prematurely.

P.S. The nicknames we gave the two men came from a book I read called `Zombie bums from Uranus`.

PPS. The children attacked their guardians – one almost pushed a guardian headfirst into the pool!

PPPS. One of the kids was paraplegic and caused a fuss.

Words are Communication Tools:

Wednesday 2/9/2020

This morning I went downstairs and did my exercise. I returned upstairs and had a shower which was sub-zero at first but 2 seconds later was harnessing the power of the sun so I could shower. After that fiasco, I got dressed and had some breakfast. Another round of typing later, I did some practise tests for my upcoming 11+ exam on the computer. Yep, just the normal working hours of this champ.

Because Mum's tummy was hurting more than usual, Dad took me to the workshop/barbershop to get my hair cut for returning to school. Whilst there, I learnt that my barber, Frankie had an accident at work. He explained that a length of pipe had fallen on his toe and broke it. It could have been worse; he said that if he were wearing the slippers he normally wore, his foot would be cut clean off. Once he completed the task of cutting my hair, he showed us a picture of his 100-year-old grandpa. This man looked like he was in his seventies.

Whilst at the swimming pool, Mum and I had a lot of fun. The pool may have been the same as the first half of my shower this morning, but it was fun. Mum got a further understanding of the breaststroke and how to use a float properly. I know, I could become a good swimming coach one day.

Thursday 3/09/2020

There was only one day left until I was in my classroom and I was calmer than I thought I would be. Usually, at the start of a new school year, I would go mad the day before and then only have a few hundred volts of energy left to get through the first day of the new school year. Today, I was as calm as a Zephyr. It was probably because I was hyped the weeks leading up to it... Hmmmmm, well, at least Mum had a lot of energy to deal with here.

As Mum and I entered the pool area at around 2:15pm, we both froze solid in the frigid water. For about 10 minutes, I sequestered myself below the surface of the water only coming up for air. I then sussed out that doing what we came to the pool to do would be a much better way of warming up. Quite a few minutes later, a man came to the pool and said the centre only wants to save money on their gas bill. I mean, not much of a surprise, is it?

For the sole reason that Mum loved pushing all the buttons, Auntie Marcia doesn't like to be pushed, we asked her when we could deliver the food for her and she was much meaner than Mum would ever be. You should have heard her rant! Wow! Her tone was just priceless...

Friday 4/9/2020

I was extremely excited that today was my first day in year 6. Not only was there the thought that I was one of the boss children of the school but a continuation of our P.E. lessons and meetings and old staff members were on the list of things that year 6 would bring. As I walked down the road leading to school my mind wandered to how Ms. Fryer would react to us. Would she even know how to handle year 6 questions? My mind was full of questions, but they were all answered as I stepped through the classroom door.

Man, Ms. Fryer was a blast! She had a very calm demeanour; my first thought was that certain kids would take advantage of this. In fact, the opposite was true. Even Henry "the horrible" who usually acted very cheekily, was a calm child today. Hurray! In art, we drew things that would remind us of COVID-19. In English, we wrote our first piece of writing to go on our `We are proud of our writing wall`. All in all, year 6 rocks!!!

On our way home, Mum gave me some fabulous news. Not only was she going to Milton Keynes to get a scan on Monday, but on Thursday, she was going to have her long awaited... SURGERY!!! This means that if all goes well, Mum would be ridded of all her pain providing more time to have fun!

Saturday 5th September 2020

Another day in my new year, I felt a bit more mature than usual. Perhaps it was because I was reading a book that I had watched in its movie form; `White fang`. Maybe it was the fact that I woke up before my Mum came into my room. But the most prominent guess of all was that I had gone through a whole 24hrs of being in year 6. Yes, my toes and right ankle may've still been aching from spending a quarter of a day wearing shoes one size too small, but I was a man now!

As you know, today was the day that I cleaned part of the house. The bathroom was the room I wanted to clean the most because I had a plan that even Einstein could not have thought up in one of his greatest brainstorms. I was going to use the vacuum that had been bought. The special close contact attachment came in very handy.

As evening dawned - no pun intended - I settled down and continued to read my book, White fang; This is a book I watched and was near the end of reading it. It is about a wolf called White fang, who gets beaten and put in dog fights before being put into the loving care of a lieutenant named Weedon Scott. For his master and his master alone, he showed great loyalty.

Another week beckons. And I felt that I had a little bit more muscle as I woke from my slumber. It might have just been my imagination but something about my calves felt a little firmer. My arms felt more compact. One thing that I kept forgetting - as usual at the start of a school year – was that I was in year 6; how do you internalise that fact? I missed out on at least one third of my penultimate year in primary school but here I was in my final year of primary school.

My weekly routine continued as I started my private karate lesson. Sensei Tyrone had agreed with Mum to tutor me on Zoom once per week. The main goal was to get me ready for my grading due to happen in a few weeks. One thing I really needed to improve was my exercise routine: sit-ups, push-ups, and leg changes. I was assured by the Sensei that I was working well, and grading would be soon. You heard that! I was nearing the point where I grade, and my blue belt would be traded for that brown belt with double white stripes...

Sometime later, I was using my tablet and thinking to myself "Alright DJ, spill the beans. What was exciting about the time you spent using the tablet?" Well, the answer is that I played very motor enhancing... games. For example, RNF4 (Rope 'n fly 4). This is a game where you use grappling hooks to swing your stick character through many famous cities. From Seattle to Chicago, so many opportunities to have fun.

It's Monday morning again and how beautiful it is. I was feeling refreshed and ready for the day ahead. After my exercise routine and an invigorating shower that scalded me, I got half-dressed and trotted downstairs for my breakfast. Once over, I started to work through my 11+ books, with such venom that you would think that I was trying to hurt someone badly. Not even a millisecond was lost but as soon as I was finished working, I was pushed out the door.

As Dad and I walked to school, we chatted about the state of the street with all the rubbish visible. We got to the gates after about twenty-five minutes and I waited to be let in at 8:30am. Dad was prepared to run to the gym as soon as I was safely inside. The was a crowd gathering at the gate and we made sure we kept our social distance.

When I arrived in my class, we were introduced to several interesting subjects. In PSHE, for instance, we did some meditation exercises; control your emotions before they control you. My English lesson was a comprehension on one of the most famous playwrights ever, William Shakespeare. In maths we ordered numbers up to 1000000 and in science we learnt about Dr. Lind's work on scurvy. That disease was so devastating in the time when the seas were the main source of long-distance travel. Trust me, it was barrels of fun.

Mum was having her CT scan today which I was hyped about; Auntie Marcia was picking me up from school and I would be going home with her. I was staying there until my parents returned home later in the evening. It was a very laid-back time; I changed out of my uniform into some more comfortable clothes and did my homework. Then I had my mouth-watering dinner which consisted of chicken, rice and curried goat, Jamaican style.

It really annoys me the way some people write up questions that even insane people would struggle to answer. Well, if you guessed that I detested them you would be wrong. Spending a lot of time thinking about the answer to an extremely hard question is not that tough to do for me. In fact, I am better at doing harder questions than easier ones. This was my morning routine in preparation for the upcoming 11+ exams.

In class I had lots of fun. We covered some great topics; in English it was expanded noun phrases, and in maths more ordering of numbers and lunch. All good stuff. Man, I loved when we had lunch; not only that but I found the first book of the series my friend Allan adored – 'Skullduggery pleasant'. Just reading one page got me falling for it hook, line and sinker. The only bad part about my school day was that it was so hot outside that we spent at least half our time at lunch lounging in the shade of the climbing area.

School had finished and Dad and I drove to Sports Direct and Decathlon where we picked up some gear for my P.E. lesson. We grabbed a jogging bottom, Tee shirt and a pair of Reeboks school shoes (my feet were being assaulted by the current one). Fun fact! I paid for all these items using Dad's card – cool! When we reached home, we saw a despondent Olivia from next door, whose leg was injured at school, and her bubbly sister Charlotte.

As I let myself into the house, I was greeted with a package that screamed "DJ... open, pleeease". There was also Mum's trademark smiley face waiting on the inside. I was bursting with excitement as I nervously opened the package, and what do I see? Nothing other than noughts and crosses, a book from Malorie Blackman.

Wednesday came around and the usual happened during the hours at home before heading off to school. I sprung out the door in my new Reeboks, which felt like they were tailored for my feet. They fit perfectly; like a hand in a glove. Apart from doing some verbal reasoning the atmosphere in the house was only barely flickering, almost dead…

Words are Communication Tools:

There were three apex moments in the school day which I am going to call the big three with no real reason in mind. Number one; we got a new (I mean old) addition to the class. None other than Nina who left in year four and was now back early this morning; on our fourth day of year 6. Number two; since I was the learning council representative in year 5, I went and had my picture taken.

I wonder if that is what Donald Trump goes through daily, man it sucks! Number three; the end of the day was manic. Both year 6 and year 5 were out on the playground at the same time in order that we could be picked up by our parents. A tidal wave of parents splashed into the playground (I did the pun by accident) Even as I am writing these sentences over two hours later, I can still hear the ringing in my ears.

You know what? I can really see why Allan (one of my best friends forever) AKA my partner in crime; loves the book series called Skullduggery Pleasant. It's about a girl called Stephanie whose uncle died. She then meets a living skeleton and along with it a whole new world of war and magic. She soon learns magic herself and hangs on with the tenacity of a dog hanging on to its bone. That's as far as I have read but I would recommend it to anyone with a good sense of humour and an appetite for magic and mystery. I couldn't wait until I got to the second book from the reading corner.

This morning I felt a little more manoeuvrable. Obviously, I was wearing a pair of jogging bottoms which gave me the ability to stretch like I have never stretched before, but there was more to it than that. I felt...I felt... I felt alive! The energy coursed through my veins as I went to school, increasing in prominence with every step taken, every road travelled, every picture Dad took of masks all over by people taking them off and dumping the road. This was the energy of confidence, and I had a lot of it!

One highlight of my school day was that we had P.E. today. This would get the average ten-year-old excited, but there was even more to the story. This was the first P.E. lesson since March of this year. We had some fun games like cups and saucers, and the one that really took the life out of me – the mile run. I think Mrs. Stef (our new P.E.) teacher underestimated how far the distance around the mound is!

Once I had gotten home, I met Kadesha (my cousin) and Auntie Marcia. About half an hour later Dad and I set off to the music academy. I met a new face at Note2note today, my new teacher Stephano. He was not at all like headteacher; in fact, he was much, much more helpful (not that the headteacher is horrible) He taught me how to strum down and up on my guitar. He also taught me how to use my picks to strum. I learnt a lot from Stephano…

Friday 11/9/2020

Pumped by the fact that we would be expected to deviate from wearing the usual school uniform for the second day.

Wednesday 16/9/2020

The best moment for the week since I was in this year group happened this morning. Forget all I said before, you are probably going to want to know why this morning was so awesome. There was one reason that made me so loquacious that even Elon, who is usually my partner in madness, could not take it anymore.

Words are Communication Tools:

For most of my journey to school I was alone. Previously the farthest I have ever gone on my own was Tufton Road and today I did not see Dad even when I got to Hampton road. I continued anyway feeling a little apprehensive with each step. Dad came running along later when I was just a few hundred meters from school. I tried to be as soft as I could to disguise my elation.

School was better than it was yesterday. That was straight to the point, wasn't it? As a matter of fact, it was several leagues above yesterday and that was down to two main events: one after the other. The first was that we had an arithmetic test that I did reasonably well in. I only dropped 8 marks in total. This was continued improvement on my tests in lockdown and maths has been oozing improvement. Maths skills aside, the final event of my day was computing.

We did some research on a so-called 'Pacific North West Tree Octopus'. We made a poster on it and at the end we typed them up. I thought it was to show how hard work feels, but Ms. Fryer then told us to rip the posters in two. It turned that the 'Pacific Northwest Tree Octopus' didn't really exist! Miss wants us to be positive and made us see how fake websites work.

Due to the hardy, durable part of my new Reeboks peeling off; Dad headed for the shops after picking me up from school. We went straight into Sports Direct to sort the matter out; under a week and the shoes were peeling.

After checking several pairs, I settled on a pair of Nikes and proceeded upstairs to do the exchange. We traded the used ones for the new ones but got nothing back and had to pay the extra. All is well that ends well, I suppose.

Yes! Words Are Wonderful.

Thursday 17/9/2020

My skin was exposed in the night because I chose to sleep without a shirt. I woke up with a nasty sore throat that made me feel like I was being stabbed with a pin in my mouth every time I swallowed. You may be thinking "OK DJ, that would only affect you when you are eating, how is it such a big problem?" Well, let me tell you that it's a lot worse than you think. For starters, every now and again, I swallow my saliva and that is agony. If that was not bad enough for you, every time I sneezed, burped or coughed my throat felt raw. We have got a lot to thank swallowing for, don't we?

I am just going to get straight to a point here; I am at school and my P.E. lesson was awesome. We may have had Mrs. Rafique when we all secretly wanted Mr. Dixon to teach us, but that did not take away from how fabulous the lesson turned out to be. We were doing football, which fitted nicely into the plan as we had the football cage today.

We concentrated on passing, intercepting, and shooting. It turns out shooting from long range was something I needed to work on because my hand-eye coordination is horrible. We did not have any matches but I was the only one to do 15 laps around the mound without stopping. You see, I told you, fun!

After I got home and did my routine; shower, dinner and then Dad and I set out for the Mount where I would have my guitar lesson. I started my second music book today and the "Boss2" made sure Dad paid for it before we left. This book taught me about quavers, which represented two notes in on beat. Along with that, I learnt a song called 'Ukraine folk song' which sounded a lot like a song I heard before. Was that memory of a song going incognito? Or is the past song incognito in the first place and Ukraine folk song was its true form?

These questions swirled in my mind as I walked home feeling as perplexed as a cat that is being neglected by its loving owner. Friday came and I woke up still feeling a tightening in my chest indicating my sore throat was still hanging around like a bad smell. I read Skullduggery pleasant before getting out of bed. It was a particularly good read and I was on the fourth volume. Called *'Dark days'*. The story so far is that Valkyrie Cain (the protagonist) rescues her partner in crime (a skeleton) that went by the name of Skullduggery from an alternate dimension. Valkyrie goes to a fortune teller who says she will fight a great war. She also finds out that her Mum is pregnant.

Fast forward to about 11:05am, and my classmates and I took a comprehension test. There were three texts: *'The lost queen'*, *'Wild Ride'* and *'Way of Dodo'*. They were not ridiculously hard and most of the class (including some of the slow ones) finished in about half an hour to forty minutes. Even though many of us had checked four times already, we had to go over the texts again and again for twenty long, agonisingly slow minutes more. Talk about punishment! We didn't even mess up behaviour wise.

Once I'd gotten home, showered and had my dinner, I went out into the fresh air of the back garden and practised pieces for the second guitar book. Do you know how good it feels to upgrade something you love? Well multiply it by 100000000000 and you have just grazed the surface of how good it felt to me. I wasn't on cloud nine nor was I on 109; I was on 10,009!

This Saturday morning, I was feeling so rough, so I slept late; something I seldom accomplish (rarely do). After a refreshing little nap, I went downstairs and finished off my homework. However, some questions were very questionable, for instance we had to learn the multiplication and division facts of our three- and 4-times table. The second thing was that we had to read for a measly ten minutes. WE read for 30 minutes in class and barely get through 14 pages. I mean, I know people have schedules, but I can assure you that 40% of the girls in my class spend hours watching Tik Tok.

By 2:02pm. Mum got a call from Allan whilst I slapped my clothes on, quick as a flash. This was all part of the master plan devised by Elon, Ellie, Tommy, and I yesterday. We were all going to meet over a video call. For some reason Elon's phone was not answered even though he was the one who proposed the idea in the first place. We all talked to Allan without Elon. He revealed to us why he has not been attending school. Ellie did not seem particularly interested, however, and was more content with saying how Tommy had supposedly burnt himself on purpose due to his burn that looked like a Nike tick. *Sigh* my friends are so strange that they are awesome.

The pandemic has really made us stop and think. It has revealed that we don't need offices. We realised the importance of a strong government to control these things and that spouting utter garbage form their mouths really does not help. It has unmasked things in the world that require urgent attention; pollution is a case. It has taught me that I can play the guitar without sounding like a strangled cat. It also made Mum explore and sharpen her baking skills. See, it appears viruses and diseases should be teachers!

My karate session on Sunday really drained my energy; they usually do though. We worked on kata mainly instead of the usual fighting aspect of the sport. Sensei said that all I really needed to work on was my balance. The competition version of Oki Nidan requires you to have the balance of a spinning top. That aside, the tutor said I was improving rapidly. When I had finished, I was so sick and exhausted I had to lie on Dad's bed and snooze.

Words are Communication Tools:

A long time later, after a shower and some minor tasks, Mum and I sat down to a most delicious meal. It consisted of sweet and sour chicken, rice, and sweet peppers. Boy was it good! Even though the chicken was still steaming when I tucked in and was through before you could say "nice food". By the end of the meal, you could have tied me to a string and used me as a balloon.

Having cleaned up the kitchen, dish washing and all, I went out into the garden and played some songs on my guitar. In fact, I was so absorbed in my task that I didn't see Olivia, her Gran and Charlotte in the garden next door. Apparently, they heard me play and came down to see the master at play. I have some fans, I believe.

Monday 21/9/2020

This morning I increased my record for walking myself to school. Heck, I even crossed the main road all on my own. A dense fog blanketed the road as I stepped out from the house. I had one thought on my mind as I rounded the corner by what used to be the library, a stone's throw from our house; it was "hot step", "hot step!". Every time I crossed the road I thought "hot brake, hot brake!" After trying and failing to cross at the pedestrian crossing three times, I made a last-ditch attempt to cross at another point and it worked.

At school in my maths lesson, Kacey and I had to join forces to solve the problems, as we used our Shanghai 6B book for the first time. You may know or not, shanghai books are notoriously hard. The question we struggled most with was one containing a flowchart. If you don't know, a flowchart is like the Maths version of personality tests in magazines. Apparently, the sums were supposed to be equal, but they were not.

Yes! Words Are Wonderful.

The session I had with my guitar today made me feel at peace with myself. It was as though I was fighting a war with myself all day. But when I played my tunes the battle ceased, you could say. As I played Ukraine folk song, the people in my mind signed a peace treaty and went back to being normal. In fact, they also joined forces.

The next morning, on my way to school, I had a funny experience. I left home around 8am as usual, told Mum and Dad I loved them and headed off into the distance. As I came off the minor roads and got to the first bus stop, I saw a familiar face. I registered the faces and my mind told me that the pair of eyes I just caught was unmistakably Hader's. We did not say anything to each other, but it was clear to me that he recognised me. A wacky encounter, I'd say.

We had a grammar test at school; like what was done last week. We were given a full hour to complete the test. Because I found it easy, I was able to finish with time to spare. I was aware because our teacher told us that about a quarter of the class never finished their work. She showed us a list but covered the names so it would be confidential.

At the end of the school day, Dad picked me up and we were home in short order. I had my shower and sat down to dinner with the family. It was chili con carne! Yes, you heard right, chili con carne; shout it from the rooftops, sing it in the square. The food critic had returned... Boy I enjoyed that meal, extra spice and all.

So, I woke up early as usual. I was out of the shower before you could say "morning routine!". This morning appeared darker than I was used to for the last few months. I guess a quarter to six in late September could be the reason. I soon worked out that winter was on its way and that could increase the risk of this Corona virus spreading. Having observed how silly some people get, little miss Corona is not exactly playing around; is it?

Later, at around 8am I talked with Dad about my task for the morning. I was about to experience something for the first time. Today I would be walking to school alone; I usually had Dad catching up before I was halfway there but today, he would not be joining me on or near Cavendish road. This morning when I got to the top of Nelson road and looked behind there was no sight of Dad on his jog.

Not only that but I was the only child there. I then had a flood of scenarios hurtling around in my mind… Am I late? Is it a school day? Am I at the wrong gate? Finally, Dad arrived as I was nearing gate #6. He explained all and congratulated me. It turns out I was exceedingly early, and his intention was to allow me to find my way.

Later, in the day, as I was on the climbing frame, I felt like the two main arm muscles near the top of my chest tore in half. I barely made it through the remainder of the day, Dad came and picked me up and I was home in a jiffy. I explained to him what I went through, and he said I should not worry, he would sort it out. I had my shower and before I knew it, Dad had boiled a new ginger concoction for me to drink and then rubbed my muscles. I felt better already. Did I tell you? I have the greatest Dad.

Another Tuesday 22/9/2020

I woke up full to the brim with energy; I leapt out of bed, regretting it almost immediately because my chest ached so much. This new chest pain made me weary of doing any serious exercise which I thought was completely understandable.

I hurried downstairs and hurriedly shovelled the breakfast down, giving the impression that I have never been fed. I was soon out the door.

School was pretty... meh for the most part. It was picture taking day and it was tedious. My picture gave the impression that I was thoroughly bored even though I tried my best not to be. We had P.E. afterwards and then the real fun started. We did passing and dribbling drills using cones and a rotary system. We moved on to 4-a side matches and I was goalie. The problem is it was biting cold and I was in school T-shirt and that added to the intensity, like rain always does a while later.

I stepped in the car to go home and saw a remarkably familiar face. It was my brother, Tore! I had not seen him for the longest time and there he was picking me up from school with Dad. We went home and later at the dinner table Tore revealed that he hadn't wanted to work as a lawyer, nor a judge nor an attorney. Man, even as he left sometime later, I was still trying to get over the pleasant shock of his initial appearance.

Friday 25/9/ 2020

Waking up, I rose out of bed like a de-glorified vampire rising out of its large coffin. I went up the stairs to my exercise routine. Wow! I did 36 push-ups instead of the usual 20 because I intended to make up for missing out yesterday. Dad always said "DJ; fitness can't be stored in the fridge". I was a little late, but it did not alter that much. Fast forward to about 8:05 am and Dad and I were in the car heading to school, the rain like dive bombing seabirds.

In class today there was a particular subject that I would like to discuss here. In our art lesson (ar'te' dessen) for French speakers. We made a collage of things to do during lockdown. Mine was in the shape of a guitar because I learnt to play the guitar during lockdown. We had all the colours we needed, as if Ms. Fryer knew what we all were thinking - as if we told her.

On arrival home today about 3:45pm, I had a plan. It was not a scrappy plan either, nor one that involved doing triple back-flips and having double flame-edged swords either. No sir! This was a plan with substance... with ...body! The plan was to take myself upstairs, grab a shower, do my homework and these very sentences. Failproof, don't you think?

Saturday is the day when I just unwind. I felt so good this morning! I had no homework; I did not have to catch up on my 11+ papers or anything of the sort. I spent most of the morning relaxing, taking my mother's advice for once☐ I slept for a while past 5:30am. Believe me when I say it felt good! By the time I started my cleaning around 11am, I was floating and finished 2hrs before I intended.

Cleaning: let us talk about that. It went far more smoothly than I thought it would. Hauling the vacuum around behind me was not keeping with the feel-good theme though. It was hectic and by the end I had a lump on my foot from it falling on it. Oh 'Henry '! - the brand of vacuum cleaner we now use. Apart from that, my session was as glassy as the Caribbean Sea.

At around 4:20pm I called up Anthony and Elon because we all certainly had some serious catching up to do. Turns out, Anthony finally got his own room and has not been back to school yet. For the rest of the call, we played truth or dare. At one point, Anthony tried persuading Elon to roll around on the floor shirtless, then Anthony ended the call so Elon and I could call Allan. He then revealed why he had not come back to school. Then we had a long conversation about Star Wars.

Yes! Words Are Wonderful.

Sunday 27/9/2020

Stretching my arms (and nearly slapping Mum across the face in the process) and unwinding with a great yawn, I trudged down the stairs, still half-asleep. To pretty much anyone who may have been watching, I seemed like I wanted my Sunday to be a lazy one. However, people who really know me would know that this phase would only last a couple of minutes. After I had my breakfast, I tore through my assessment like a road runner.

Karate this morning was a blast. Of course. I was so weak that a leaf could knock me over by the end of it, but that was the whole point of my karate workouts! We made some particularly good progress this lesson. The main part of it was spent learning the first three moves of Oki Yodan. This was the final kata and the official longest in history. Man was it hard!

Tore's unexpected visit on Thursday had spurred me to use Duolingo a lot more. That was because Tore's daily streak was 280 days. If that wasn't enough his mother's streak was in the 650s! If that's not dedication I do not know what is! I had seen Tore's Duolingo screen and it is full of gold images (which means mastery). Seriously though, if you saw the screen, you'd think Tore's been speaking Spanish all his life! He was great, so I could only begin to comprehend how gold his Mum's screen was!

Monday 28/9/ 2020

I was full of beans this morning because today was my mother's birthday! I came downstairs to a bouquet of flowers and blue lights on the big mirror behind the dining table. Mum was in the kitchen cooking up a storm, I thought to myself "why is poor Mum working on her birthday?" I was about to ask her, when I remembered all the past times, I had asked her the question. She would always answer "do you see anyone else doing it?" At least we got a breakfast!

The normal routine at school had not changed much; the only difference was that lunchtime, all the boys (including me) ate in a food frenzy. It's not like I was in any shape to play football in the first place. Moving my arms too much or running too fast causes an immense amount of pain in my chest. For the whole of lunch time, I just played Catch with Mr. Barker and Darrell who is another year Six boy.

As you have already found out in my first paragraph, today was my mother's birthday. It was when I got home from school that the real party began. Auntie Marcia was there when I got home and very shortly after that, my cousin Kadesha came along. Not long after that we all sat down to a delightful meal with everything from prawns to salad, rice to both jerk and fried chicken. Mum said that starting from tomorrow, we will all have to shed some pounds. Dad we might have to roll ourselves to bed.

Tuesday 29/9/ 2020

Remember those chest pains I told you about? They are back and more intense than before. As I took the stairs to do my exercise, it dawned on me that I would struggle royally, whilst going through my routine. I wanted to writhe on the floor as I started my sit-ups. The pain was so much I went down the stairs in short order. I grabbed my shower, relishing the warmth of it, relaxing my muscles. I struggled to get my clothes on without having sharp pain, I did my CGP work and was out the door faster than you could say "rainy day".

My school day descriptions will have at least 3 positives. Positive #1 – I had a blast outside playing the most painless game of catch ever; I didn't get bonked on the bounce or hit in the unspeakable area! Positive #2 – I had such a good lunch due to Tommy being the first person to ever ask to sit next to me. Positive #3 – I drew one of the cutest pictures of a baby sea turtle that I have done in a long time. Dad and I have been working on this idea of teasing out three positives for everyday as soon as I come out of school.

I had gotten home and was playing the guitar in front of a live audience. It was outside and it could have been Olivia (who called herself Margaret) and Charlotte (calling herself Karen), but it was an audience, nonetheless. At the end of it, Charlotte ran around screaming "I am Karen!!!" but Oliva seemed genuinely impressed, an exceedingly rare spectacle.

The next morning, I left the house on a high note; I did very well in the maths test I had done earlier in the day. I stepped out the house covered in my coat, scarf, and hood. The slightly miserable weather did not hinder my pace in the slightest. If anything, it motivated me to increase my step! Even more than usual; due to this fact, I was walking to school on my own for the second time.

Positives for today; shortened as the 3 Ps is coming to you once again. I dropped only one mark in my reasoning paper; learnt about Python code in computing and running around more today than I did yesterday and there were many others. It is so much easier to be positive than negative. In fact, it takes more effort to frown than to smile…

I had gotten inside, flung my bag down and flew up the stairs in a rush to get through what I needed to do. This was because

I needed to get my practise test done. I finished the test and got a half-decent score of 43. It was a good starting point, but my Dad said that the minimum was 47 to get through. Even so, at least I did not fail.

Thursday 1/10/ 2020

First day of the second month in my final year in primary school; sounds poetic. I did another assessment test from the maths test pack. Once the test started, my mind was still unfocussed, which showed in my results; two less than my tests yesterday in fact. I got 82% correct, and the minimum passing grade was 85%. Considering how I had only completed 2 tests; it was a great score!

I am only going to be talking about my P.E. lesson today. For the most part, it had a satisfactory lesson, akin to that of having a brand-new friend. My trainers may have been squeezing my feet like a vice; OK, so that is an exaggeration, but my chest felt like it was about to tear open when I did my daily mile. I had a lot of fun doing it anyway and that is all that counted.

A couple of hours later, I was sauntering out of the house and into the music academy centre. I played some new and enjoyable songs such as Pierre Jacques, Polish dance and La Mantoventa. Coming out of the music room, the man at the desk said that I was 'Top boy'. It was a nice comment and made better by the man telling my Dad!

Yes! Words Are Wonderful.

Friday 2/10/ 2020

Two major things happened this morning which was made it feel more official than usual. The first thing here was the fact that I did my 3rd 11+ test. The score of 42 yesterday was an incentive to work harder than ever before. The second major thing was that I received a pair of Dad's pants in a very sacred ritual!

Trapped inside the school due to an immense amount of torrential rain, I had an expectable and equally as annoying lunch break. Not only were all the GGs (Gossip Girls) using all their power to... well, gossip, but Ms. Fryer had to search the deepest reaches of Netflix to find a rated movie that most people had not watched. Much to my surprise, most people had not watched `Willy Wonka`, which was the chosen movie!

Fast forward to 20 minutes to five and Dad and I looked over where I went wrong in my 11+ test. I got 44/50; this was my highest so far. Dad opened my eyes to a whole new way of looking at questions. For the most part; it's about the process. An example is that you can't get to school unless you leave your house; you must start from the beginning and proceed from there.

Saturday 3/10/ 2020

I woke up and stretched my limbs which were so achy you would have thought that I was asleep for 9 months, not hours! Feeling the usual waves of grogginess cascade over me like a waterfall, I trudged into the spare room, where Mum quickly told me to go back to bed; it was only 4 in the morning. Waking up and stretching (again) I was ready to take on my day, along with the two assessments that awaited me.

Nine o clock came around and it rained like no one's business! As I came upstairs to do my routine cleaning job, the sound of the rain on the roof was thunderingly loud and almost… almost protective. What I meant was that the rain made me feel comforted and secure. Sure, there may have been amber weather warning in some parts of the county but, hey!

Later in the day, I did my 4th maths test, and it was the worst test outcome so far. I will avoid beating around the bush; I will say it out loud and proud and up front I got 41/50. The sole reason for the bulk of my test was that I by myself. Usually, I zone out and Mum would snap me out of it. This time, there was no one else but me! I really need to up my game, I thought to myself.

Sunday 4/10/ 2020

This morning, I had my mind dead set on one thing: work. I worked through my little exercise in my verbal reasoning and maths taking notes on them of time. When I was halfway through my maths, I sighed inwardly because next week would be nothing like this one; we would only be patching up my pitfalls.

A little while later, I was doing my karate lesson. I learnt a few things including how to duck and weave as an evasive manoeuvre, but we got the next move: the Oki Shodan. There were a lot more things going on in the lesson as well.

Fast forward to around 4:22pm and my barber, Frankie was cutting my hair, and during this process Manchester United was getting its butt kicked by Liverpool. Dad and Frankie were both intently watching not on the little TV over his head but on his phone. Imagine having a man cut your hair whilst he and another are saying how Man U were idiots.

October 5/10/ 2020

This morning was one in which I unlocked a new ability. I call it instant transmission (not to be mistaken with transmission from Dragon ball Z) but if it sounds too cheesy, I will not change it because that's my choice to make and I am not changing it for anyone but me, myself and I. It all started when I was walking to school. I felt droplets of water on my palms and I knew I had to act fast. With a burst of speed rivalling Usain Bolt, I got to school in record time. Thus, instant transmission was born! See, you can do anything if you try!

After lunch I had a pleasant surprise. I stepped into the classroom, only to see Mr. Dixon (he sometimes teaches maths and P.E.) Moreover, he was going to be there for the remainder of the day. Just in case you missed it earlier, Mr. Dixon is the only Jamaican teacher I know outside of my mother and father, but he is also the maths whiz in Selwyn primary. Yeah! I know, it is amazing!

School was over and I had reached home. I had my dinner when it happened. I was playing the guitar as I do these days as a matter of habit, I realised what my cousin Kashief meant when he spoke to me yesterday. If you want to know what he said, it is the following "A piece of music seems a lot better if it has a story behind it". I played a song which shall remain anonymous and I made up a story behind it. I said it was played by a Mexican woman forced to marry an arrogant snob. I played it again and it sounded a lot better because I knew why the notes were used in certain places in the song.

Words are Communication Tools:

Tuesday 6/10/ 2020

Another early morning: whilst it was still dark outside, I was washing away the dirt and sleep of the morning and preparing for the day ahead. I went down the stairs with a pep in my step, hastily prepared and gulped down my cereal before doing another practise paper. After about an hour I was stepping out the door and motoring down the road like a powerboat.

I felt like I had a motor housed in me that was carrying me down the street. The cool air calmed my mind, getting me ready for the day. As I rounded the last corner and turned onto Selwyn Avenue, I felt Dad approaching on his jog.

The school day was a great deal more entertaining thanks to one key thing – the first ever learning council meetings held this morning. Mr. Livie and Mrs. Wagner (Isabelle's Mum) were there, and they asked us questions like "Do you feel safe?" and "How has the timetable been altered?" Now that I really look back at it, there were only three pupils there who were at least 10; all the other were as young as seven. At the end, I learnt we were going to the learn about archery, with real weapons… Not the suction arrows I have at home. These were real flint-tipped arrows.

Once again, I am talking about the art of playing the guitar. This time, I am talking about the song 'Frere Jacques' and 'Salmonella Tuna'. It reminded me of a Rocksteady leaflet. It said, 'try altering the words of the song!' I did, and it was HILARIOUS!!! Before I finish, please note I have left Rocksteady… I now attend the weekly lesson at 'Note-2-Note' in a building on the High street of my town.

Yes! Words Are Wonderful.

Wednesday 7/10/2020

Bang on 5:45am, I was up in my parents' room completing my routine exercises; drills included: forty second planks, push-ups, sit-ups, Ak strikes and a whole lot more... My shower was made relaxing due to the steam; not, of course, the scalding water pouring out of the shower. I came downstairs, had my breakfast, and revised some maths and VR (short for verbal reasoning) before motoring off to school.

Fast forward to around 2:05pm and we had a maths and computing mash-up. The idea was to have half the class work on their own, plan for an option-based adventure game, whilst the other half took down some negative number questions.

I was in the half working on the game in computing and I based my game/story on a book I read and own called 'The legend of Zelda: ocarina of Time'. In my plan, you are attacked by a foul beast who was half-man, half-hog. You can either attack with a sword (and then purify him or die) or protect using a shield (then call your swordsman master friends or die!). Yep, there's a lot of death going on, but `The Legend of Zelda` is awesome like that.

I would like to discuss the book I am currently reading, called (COGHEART). It's about a girl called Lilly Hartman who is the daughter of a world-renowned robot inventor. He suddenly disappears, proclaimed dead, making Lily find her life turned onto its head. Her 'guardian' strips the house to find any riches Mr. Hartman may have left behind. I would recommend it to anyone who has even the slightest sense of humour because this book is comedy gold!

Thursday, 8/10/2020

I completed another mock 11+ exam this morning; it was of the English variation. It was a great deal more laid back (I'm trying so hard not to use the word easy), which proved itself when I got 90% out of 54 correct! The work included: a comprehension about an extract from the book `Swiss Family Robinson', a book I had eyes on; a spelling test and a grammar test. I think I was grafting!

Once 13:05 rolled around, we played a game called `*Musical Hoops* for our first part of P.E. It's pretty much Musical Chairs, but you must stand in hoops instead of sitting on chairs. I came first in the first two rounds but came second to Arthur in the last round, due to me falling. We then headed out to the playground and completed our daily mile. Overall rating: 12.5/10!

My guitar lesson consisted of me learning to play two strings at once, that old strings snap a lot easier, new chords and much more besides. I was praised for my work.

Friday, 9/10/2020

I was grouchy this morning, causing my patience to split in half, and I guessed most of my answers. By the end of it, my morale and patience had reached the pits. I was told by Mum not to worry, though I did exactly that. I thought that Tia was rubbing off on me; she's a pessimist and she sits near me in class.

A long while later, we had an Art lesson all about optimism, so that lifted my spirits a bit. We had to paint a background, though we could only use colours that reminded us of Lockdown. We then had to write a positive saying. I had a sort of misty background because the rain in lockdown looked more beautiful than usual. Also, Dad and I had been ambushed by it multiple times when out exercising. I then wrote about being in a good place mentally.

I was mid-way through my homework when Allan called. I had heard the news from Ms. Dunne, but it was no less sweet to hear it from the man himself. The all-important news is that Allan is only mild risk, so he can come back to school on Monday! That would certainly make the most boring day of the week better!

Sunday, 18/10/ 2020

This morning, I woke up, stretched my limbs and almost struck Mum across the face. It took me a few moments to realise that Mitri was sleeping in the spare room, Mum's usual camp out. At around 9:15am, I was in the loft, starting my weekly karate session with Sensei Tyrone. This week's session came armed with good news. Sensei said that in the half-term, I'd be able to do my grading. "ABOUT TIME!" I thought to myself. Took over a year for it to happen, but it finally happened. I was so excited, I trundled through my lesson like a bulldozer.

After my lesson, I had a much-needed shower, then came downstairs and logged onto Google Classroom to get my homework done. The only problem was, I could only see last week's homework. So, I called one of my best friends and Google Classroom guru, Allan. Whilst he walked it through with me, I introduced him to Mitri for the first time. She showed off her… unique humour, like Allan's and mine. Allan then made us all want to roll about laughing by talking about the low-level quality of our homework. In fact, his sister answered most of the questions!

At 6pm, Tore finally turned up, so we could tuck into the meal prepared for us by Master Chef Mum. The adult conversation was like one of those weird talk shows, where the host interviews people and they say something that makes everyone laugh. They're a queer bunch, adults are.

Monday, 19/10/ 2020

I felt like a real boss when I entered the shower after my exercise this morning. I guess I should better explain. With a blazing aura of confidence, I went up into the loft and did my exercise. I then did 10 push-ups straight – twice! The Boss is back!

Our Science lesson today made school particularly interesting. We didn't look at the elements of the Periodic Table, as epic as that would've been. Instead, we looked at the classification of living things. We drew a table and ordered living things like toadstools and jellyfish into it. It was oodles of fun! Ms. Fryer asked us if we knew the difference between plants and animals and I broke down the concept of cell walls for the class!

Fast-forward to a quarter to 6 and I was using Yousician (not an advert, by the way) and looked at the vast expanse of songs at my disposal. Well… they weren't so much at my disposal, because all the songs I did and didn't want to play were premium, which, of course, you must pay for. Even 'Redemption Song' was there, but it was premium too! Ugh!

Yes! Words Are Wonderful.

Tuesday, 20/10/ 2020

I had another wonderfully tiring exercise session, then let my muscles relax in the cascading waterfall that was my shower. My whole kit for school was prepared by me, then I sat in front of the computer, engraving the first 10 elements into my brain. Soon, it was 8am and I was rocketing down the road to school.

School, for the most part, was a bit of a drag. Science was fine; we did some more classification. Grammar, however, mmm... not so much. Maths was about perimeter and area, which wasn't all that hard. R.E was about the Buddhist 'Triple Jewel',

which wasn't great and wasn't horrible. Overall, if my day were a sound, it would be a *'meh'*.

At half past 5pm, I was taking great difficulty in combing Mum's hair, which was full of the remnants of her hair gel. I was telling her about life in Year 6, and she was telling me that we were *'getting back to work'* in the half term, and that Dad would chip in with some science too! That would be awesome!

Wednesday, 21/10/2020

I broke my record of most push-ups done at once; this time, I did twelve! Even though I knew that I could do much better, I was happy, nonetheless.

School was supposedly a great time. That was true for me, at least up until lunchtime. As you may know, Wednesday afternoons are a mix'n'mash of computing and maths. Because the computers weren't working, Ms. Fryer let us have a half-hour of free time on the tablets. Sadly, a certain Max and Henry had put so many pictures of stupid things on the tablet, that I only got a 3rd of the time we were given to do anything I wanted!

Let me now talk about my Headteacher's behaviour when we were outside, waiting to get picked up from school by our parents. Before I continue, let me just add that it was pouring with rain this day. He was almost idly walking into the playground in the vaguest direction of the school gates. He then backtracked and talked and joked with all the teachers, before just standing, almost a still taunt, looking at the miffed parents, for at least 7 minutes. I mean, come on! You're supposed to be in control! I expect you to use your authority to sort things out!

Thursday, 22/10/2020

The last day of school had finally come along, bringing Pink for Breast Cancer Day with it. Instead of the normal P.E kits, we were allowed to wear a pink item of clothing as well. *Sarcasm right here* Yay! I walked so fast to school, that I was the first one there out of all of Year 6! Yep, I'm that fast.

The P.E lesson was a blast; at least, for everyone but poor Allan. He had to have restrictions on his exercise due to him being mild risk. He also had to face the, as he called it, "Short tempered Dragon" A.K.A Mrs. Rafique. He could only be a referee in the 4-a-side match we had, and the daily mile. This put a weight on his usually jolly nature, which Elon, Tommy, Ellie, and I tried to lift.

My usual guitar lesson wasn't at all usual. In fact, one of the songs Stephano and I played sounded a lot like a song I'd heard. The title was *'New World Theme'*, which sounded a lot like an ad I see on the way to school, but that's *'Brave New*

World'. Either way, it brushed against and stirred up something... familiar.

Friday, 23/10/2020

The first day of the Half-Term was simply fine. In the early morning, I wrote about the differences between plants and animals. Once I had gotten to the second and final point (that plants have a cell wall and animals don't), I treated myself to some toast for breakfast and a break. I thought to myself that life was awesome as I sat in the settee, watching *'Bondi Vet'*.

Ms. Fryer hosted the first ever Year 6 parents' evening at 1pm. She was in the classroom, which, for some reason, gave it a homely feel. She talked about my pros and cons in the classroom, then went on to explain my *quote unquote* "Student contract". It was pretty much that I needed to work on when and when not to shut up.

When I practised playing my guitar, I discovered this wonderful thing called TAB. TAB has six lines on it, representing the six strings. The numbers on the lines represent the fret. I would recommend it to any budding guitarist who wants to learn songs quickly.

Saturday, 24/10/2020

I did a lot of reading this morning. I read about the struggles of hosting a theatre show, and some of Houdini's most famous daredevil exploits. Huh. No wonder it's called *'How is it done?'*.

I went on another errand toady; this time to retrieve some pumpkin from Auntie Marcia. It was a blustery, miserly sort of day. Mum gave me her baggy jumper to wear. On the way, I whistled the Pokemon theme song, warming me up a little.

I watched the Second `Home Alone` movie, full of grown criminals getting burnt, beaten, and generally bullied by the same 10-year-old from last Christmas. My rating: 10/10!

Sunday, 25/10/2020

I had read so much over the past three days that my eyes had started to strain! The pitter-patter of rain had very quickly turned from a comfort to a nuisance; it had gotten very loud, thick, and fast. I put my earphones on at one point because it at least muffled the relentless beat of drums that was the torrential downpour.

You must be wondering how my karate lesson went. You could say that it went "swimmingly" (no pun intended). It was raining for most of the lesson, which was bad for sensei due to him being in his local park. He eventually put his umbrella over his computer, meaning that a bit of fabric hung over his screen for most of the lesson! *Sigh*.

The afternoon was... meh. I played some guitar and watched some people play guitar. I watched TV and eventually the TV watched Mum sleep. I ate some food without it eating me. I drank some water without it using me to quench its thirst. See? I could've been dead by now! My life is a danger hazard!

Yes! Words Are Wonderful.

Monday, 26/10/2020

I woke up this morning, reeking of sweaty socks and Canadian Healing Oil. The reason for this is that I had Canadian Healing Oil on my sore big toe (it was ingrown) and I had a sock on top of it. I did 40 half-push-ups due to my toe (double my usual 20) and, after a nice hot jet of water cascaded over me, I was good for the day!

Mum and I decided that it was time to put some work in; I had 2 days of work lost. We were going to work through Mum's huge tome of practise SATs papers, but we focused on translation and reflection. I only dropped marks because I reflected the wrong way but was otherwise fine.

After some tunes were strummed on my guitar, I looked at the real-life version of ultra-instinct (a form in Dragon Ball Super), the flow state. The flow state is a state of mind in which you lose all perception of time or anything around you; you're only conscious of what you're doing. You wouldn't know it's happened until you've come out of it because you wouldn't be able to realise you are in it when you are in it.

Tuesday, 27/10/2020

Another day, another cycle of waking up when my alarm goes off only to realise that I was an hour early. I woke up (again) an hour later and dutifully completed my 20 push-ups. I did 19, then 1, not the whole set, but better than yesterday's set.

At 12:30, the doorbell rang and I, unofficially being the friendly household door-answerer, opened the door. There was a parcel which contained nothing other than a brand-new guitar case, complete with pick holders and a place for books. It even had straps, making it a half-backpack, half-guitar case! So cool!

At around quarter past 1pm, Mum asked me to retrieve my dinner from Auntie Marcia. When I got there, I wasn't the slightest bit surprised that Auntie Marcia hadn't even cooked yet. So, I waited there for about 2 hours before walking back home. I spotted a boy on his bike staring at me, but I just continued on my way. When I got to Marmion Avenue, who was pedaling beside me but the boy from down the road! He enquired why I looked at him. Jeez! Why'd he need to know? Did he just go up to every person who looks at him and try to threaten him?!?!?!

Wednesday, 28/10/2020

This morning, we dropped Mum off at Whipps Cross hospital and waited for her to come out. We left at about 7:00am, tried to go off in Dad's silver Lexus, which failed to start. Thankfully, that wasn't the only car in the house, and we went out in Blueberry, Mum's blue Honda. On the way, we heard something strange on the news, which was that Kier Starmer, the leader of the Labour party had an accident with a cyclist whilst on the road. I mean, come on! Bit random, isn't it!

There wasn't any room designated for waiting, so Dad and I camped out in the car. After what seemed like 15 eternities, but was only 15 minutes, Dad and I went out to a marsh in a neighbouring spot near Dad's parking slot. There was a lake in the marsh, full of Coots, Canada geese, seagulls, mallards and even Sky Rats (err... I mean... pigeons) flocking to the waters to feast on stale bread chucked in by laughing spectators. In no time, we had to go and pick-up Mum.

When we finally got home, I emptied the bottle I had… urinated in on the journey, before settling down, to a few relaxing levels of Wordscapes. There were some strange words like 'herr' and 'rue'. I knew that to rue meant to hate, but I had to look up the meaning of 'herr' (apparently, this is the German standardisation of a man, kind of like calling someone Sir).

Thursday 29/10/2020

This morning, once I had done my exercise and had my shower, it was my idea that it would be another laid-back day. Unfortunately, I was completely and utterly on the ball. It was starting to get annoying, not being able to go outside that often; we are in lockdown. At least, I still had my music lessons to look forward to, which would break up the monotony of being stuck indoors.

This is a 'Thank You' to all YouTube artists, who help rookie artists like me, draw something half-decent. What makes me feel small, compared to you people, is that some of you draw in Sharpie, which is a permanent marker. Even still, you use such quick strokes sometimes; that really make me look on with bated breath.

The time whizzed by and after what seemed like half-an-hour, I was speeding down the road, hell-bent on getting to my guitar lesson, in the five minutes I had, 'till it started. Once I got there, I had to navigate through the narrow warren of corridors, whilst walking side-ways like a crab, due to my cumbersome guitar case (which funnily was wider than the corridor).

Friday 30/10/2020

I had a little spike of energy this morning; we (Dad and I), had our first Book Camp session today! With an extra spring in our step, I bounded downstairs and quickly gobbled my bowl of heavenly oats porridge. I wanted to be ready for the session, so I could make my grand entrance into the world of book writing!

From 10:00 – 12:00 noon, Dad tutored one of his students, so I was left to my own devices once again (Mom was out doing the weekly food shop). To occupy myself, I engaged in a spot of drawing and some guitar playing, before watching an engaging documentary by David Attenborough. An hour-and-a-half later, Mom returned from her shopping trip and it was time for the Book Camp.

APOSTROPHES:

Apostrophes are easy to understand. However, knowing when to use them can be a challenge.

Apostrophes can be used to contract words (shorten them). Imagine you are at a beach and a man is calmly paddling in the sea. Suddenly, a shark appears out of the water! The lifeguard shouts "Do not worry! There is 100% not a shark swimming behind you!"

Try contracting "do not". You'd (See? Used one!) get rid of the `o` and replace it with an apostrophe. That would be `don't`. Unfortunately, the English language can be really annoying sometimes and there are homophones like 'you're' and 'your'. I get this wrong so many times and the English language pretty much accepts it now, but it's apparently good to know the proper way.

'You're' is a contraction for 'you are', so you would say it in a sentence like "You're doomed; the school bullies are going to open a portal and throw you into it!" However, 'your' is a possessive pronoun, so you would use it like "It's your fault, Danielle!" I know, the English language is really complicated.

IMAGERY:

METAPHORS:

Metaphors are phrases that don't literally mean what they say. If you said, "The dragon's horns were a pair of yellow spires", you don't mean that a dragon had a pair of yellow spires casually sticking out of its head, do you? It means that the horns were a very rotten shade of yellow and awfully long. It's a way of making you think of two things at once.

IMAGERY:

PERSONIFICATION:

Personification is like a poetic metaphor. It describes things incapable of having thoughts or feelings (the weather, for example) as if it could have thoughts and feelings. For example, "The sea thrashed about. It roared and beat at the sand and nearby cliffs". That's personification; the sea can't just waltz up and thrash about.

Examples of Imagery:

Entry level:

- The wind raged.
- The car was a ripe banana.

Intermediate level:

- The moon is an enormous silver eye.
- The sun pierced me like a bright hot arrow.
- The oceans are giant splodges of paint.

Yes! Words Are Wonderful.

Mastery level:

- Life is a journey.
- The engine roared into life.
- The train chugged along happily.

FINAL QUIZ:

This is the last quiz in this book. Have fun! There are 5 questions this time!

1) What could metaphors be used commonly in?

   a) banana splits

   _____

   _____

   b) milkshakes

   _____

   _____

   c) poems

   _____

   _____

APOSTROPHES:

2) Use three metaphors to describe the moon.

   _____

   _____

   _____

3) List three personification phrases

   _____

   _____

4) Make the sentence "she had lovely hair" better using imagery.

   _____

   _____

5) What is imagery's purpose?

   _____

   _____

Nice work getting through all those questions!

Finally, you can call yourself a proper wordsmith!

Yes! Words Are Wonderful.

Afterword by Derrick H. Shortridge Sr.

DJ opened this book with a quotation by the late Nelson Mandela "All is impossible until someone does it".

I passionately believe that through literacy we can change the world. Greta Thunberg has shown that young people have the power to make that change and I am determined to contribute to the process. The planet needs us; we are going to need it to live on for much longer than the older people. If we continue to read and understand the way it works, we will be better able to take care of it.

The way of getting the key information out is through reading and comprehension. The national curriculum in KS2 in the UK has led on this, by having teaching material produced on the subject. Children who cannot read and write will miss this and other crucial messages. We need to teach our children the basics about climate change, and the inspirational student, aiming to raise awareness of it by using these differentiated reading comprehension activities, which are perfect for most pupils across the world.

For those who might utilise these resources, they are split into three different ability levels: entry, intermediate and mastery. It is ideal for tailoring your lessons to each individual child's capabilities.

Don't quit reading!

Even when your child can read on their own, they still benefit from the connections you help them make when you read together. We are promoting reading aloud to children well into their teen years. Derrick has read the Harry Potter series; some hefty volumes, I observed.

He has wonderful conversations about writing, ethics, and connections to experiences the teenagers were having in school because he speaks so well with people older than he is.

My suggestion is that you do whatever works for your family to make reading fun and engaging. This way, the current generation and future generations will be much more literate. When children grow up, adults still have a pivotal role to play in how they feel about reading and learning.

As we train them to develop empathy, associating reading with good times, and bad, your children and young adults will gain a new perspective on life. The world needs a literate population, and we can only achieve that through wordsmithery....

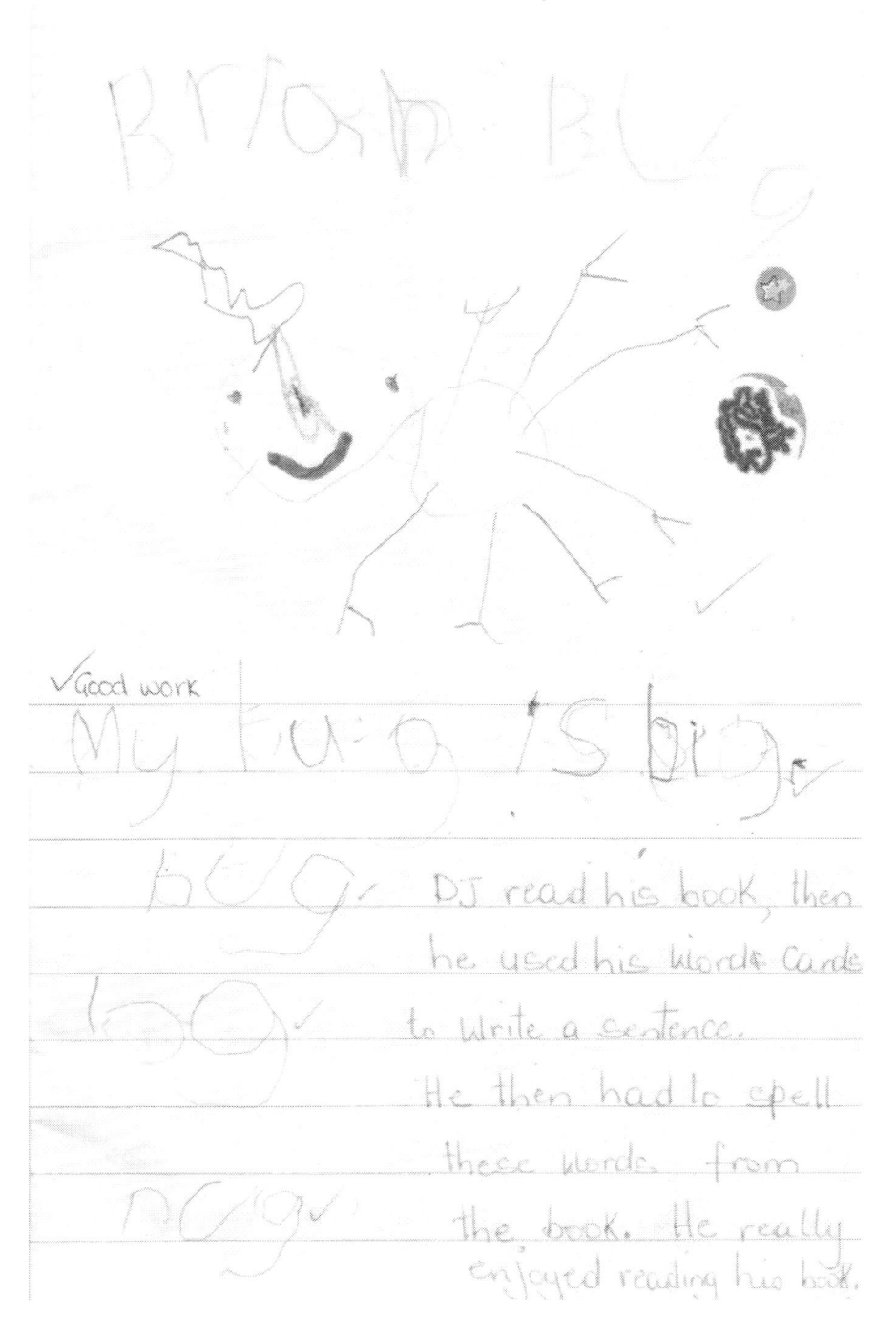

Yes! Words Are Wonderful.

Some of my early work

✓ Good work

My two is big

big. DJ read his book, then
he used his words cards
to write a sentence.
He then had to spell
these words from
the book. He really
enjoyed reading his book.

✓ Good work Derrick

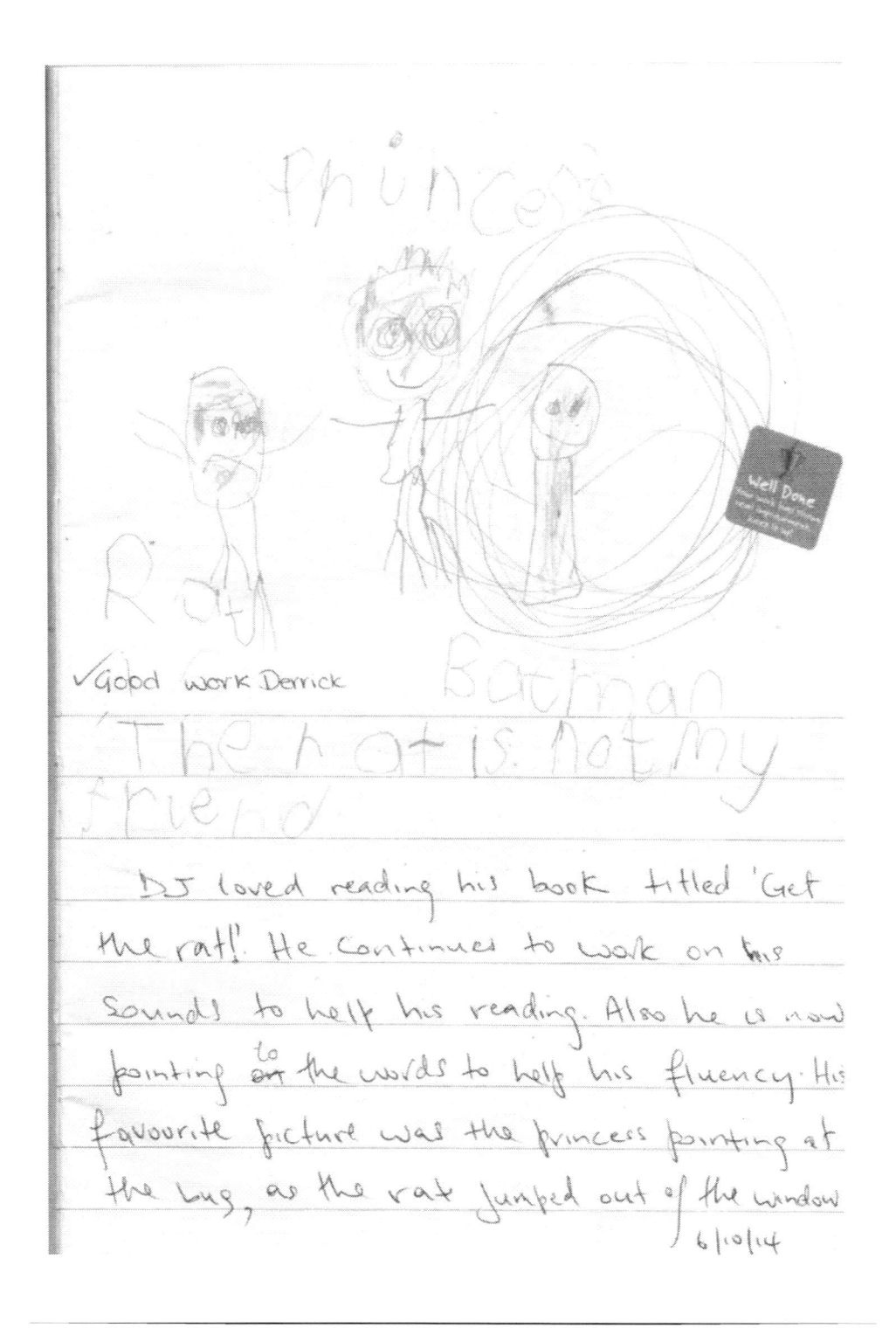

'The rat is not my friend'

DJ loved reading his book titled 'Get the rat!'. He continues to work on his sounds to help his reading. Also he is now pointing to the words to help his fluency. His favourite picture was the princess pointing at the bug, as the rat jumped out of the window

6/10/14

Yes! Words Are Wonderful.

A robin's egg   Jan 20, 2015

The robin is really great.
The eggs are blue.

Some of my early work

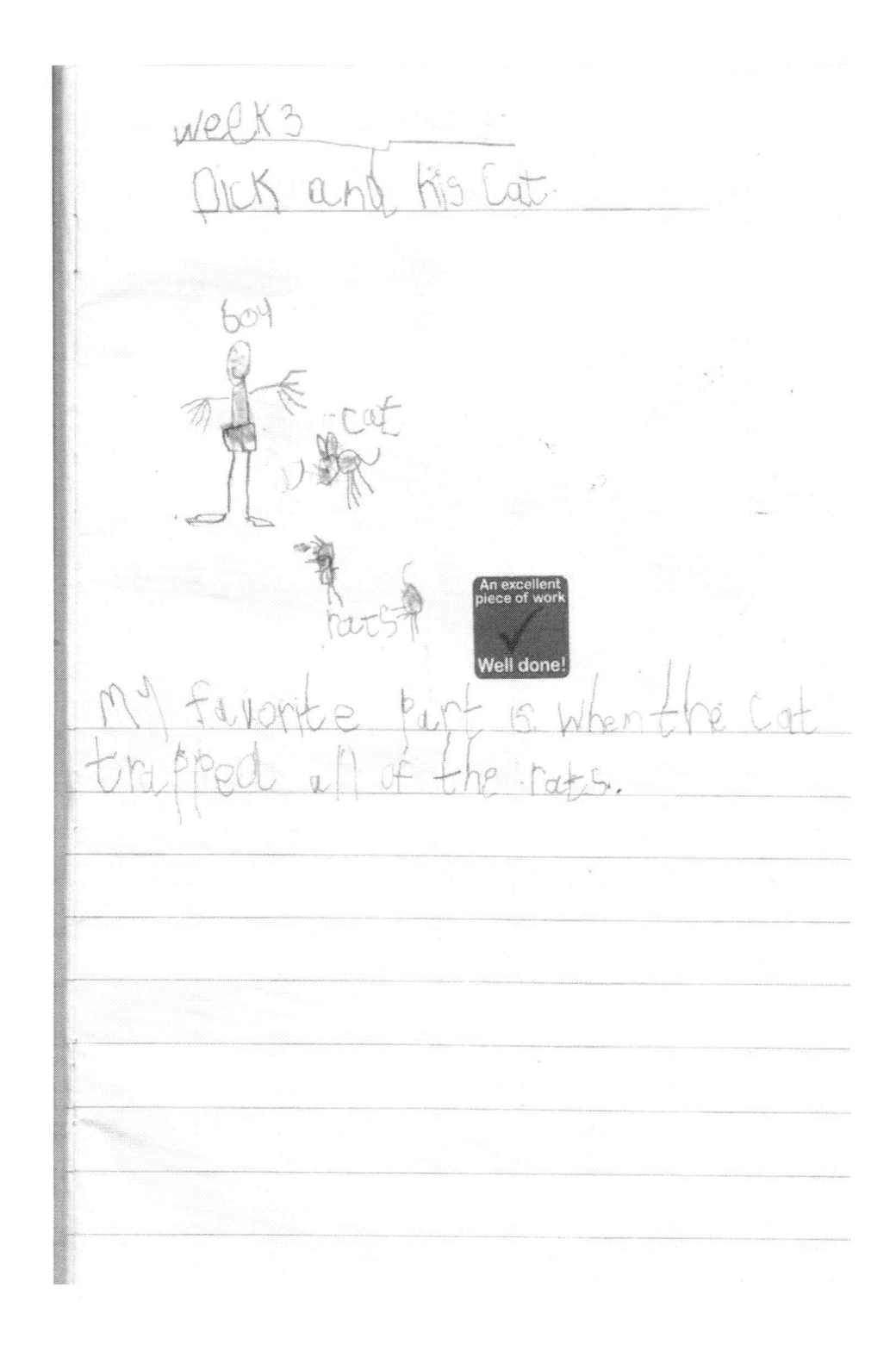

week 3
Dick and his cat

[child's drawing of a boy, a cat, and rats, with labels "boy", "cat", "rats", and a teacher's sticker reading "An excellent piece of work — Well done!"]

My favorite part is when the cat trapped all of the rats.

Yes! Words Are Wonderful.

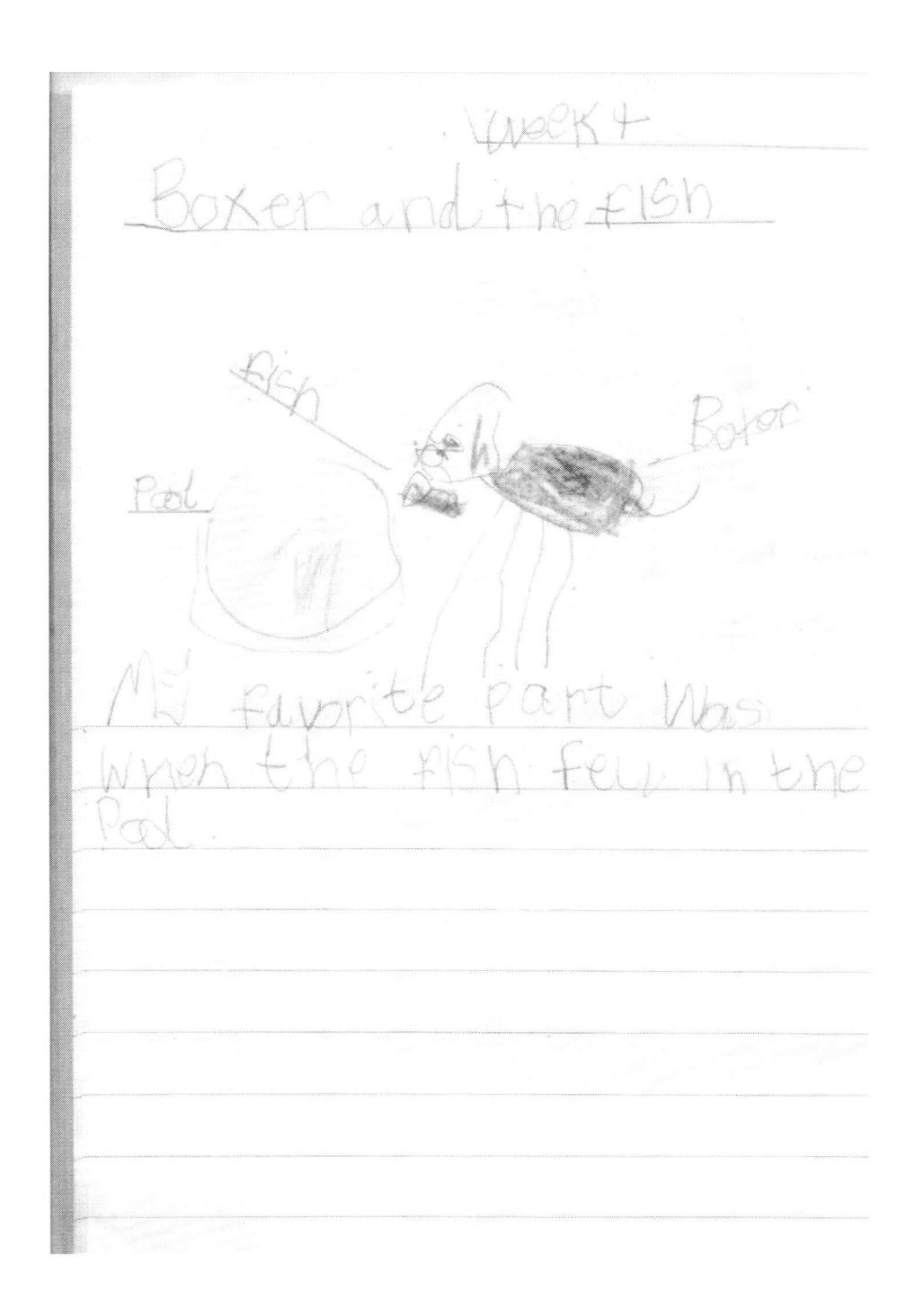

Week 4
Boxer and the fish

My favorite part was when the fish fell in the pool.

Some of my early work

A bars in the night
week 5
24/3/2015

tent

burrow

ruff

dog

my favorite was the owl because I have owl eyes

Yes! Words Are Wonderful.

NOTES:

Introduction:

1. American Academy of Pediatrics

2. www.healthychildren.org

3. `Wildlife of Britain; A Unique Photographic Guide to British Wildlife`; DK

4. "*How is it done?*"; Reader's Digest

5. `*The Bible for Minecrafters*`, Christopher Miko, Garrett Romines

6. `*1001 secrets every birder should know tips and trivia for the backyard and beyond*`, Sharon "Birdchick" Stiteler

7. `*Beyond Bedtime Stories, 2nd. Edition: A Parent's Guide to Promoting Reading Writing, and Other Literacy Skills from Birth to 5, (2014)* ` by Susan Bennett-Armistead, Ph.D. and Gabriel Civiello, M.D. (excerpted from 'Building Brains by Making Connections,' published in Parent & Family, March 2, 2016

Printed in Great Britain
by Amazon